Ms. Dorothy

It has been
Pleasure meeting

Bullet Proof

May God continue
to bless you on your
journey

May you be inspired to tell
your story, even after
reading mine!

God Bless 2019

MW00679109

Bullet Proof

BODIE QUINETTE

ISBN: 978-0-9980148-0-7
Library of Congress Control Number: 2017938781

Designed and Published by:

The Solid Foundation Group, LLC
PO Box 1483
Smyrna, GA 30081
www.TheSolidFoundationGroup.com

Printed in the United States of America

**...Weeping may endure for a night,
but joy cometh in the morning.**

Psalm 30:5 (KJV)

Dedication

This book is being dedicated to my husband, sons, mother, sister, brothers, closest family and friends, and all of those persons who have found and/or find themselves going through similar struggles.

Trust in the Lord with all your heart,
and lean not unto your own understanding.
In all your ways, acknowledge Him, and
He shall direct your paths. (Prov. 3:5-6)

Acknowledgements

From what started as a creative thought in my mind to now being a published work of art, I must take a moment to acknowledge all of those who have helped make what used to be just a dream a now pleasant reality:

To God, my first love, I say thank you for blessing me with the vision, talent and testimonies needed to compose and complete this project. It hasn't been an easy journey; but, I'm thankful, nonetheless, for I know it was Your perfect will and favor over my life that made it all possible.

Secondly, I'd like to acknowledge and thank my husband and sons for their unwavering love, support and creative energy. To my mother, sister, brothers, aunts, uncles, cousins, and a host of other relatives and close friends, including my late grandmother, Carrie, grandfather, Eugene, uncle, Raymond, and aunt, Mary – thank you all for a consistent and constant flow of love and support over the years.

Special thanks also go to all of those who believed in me and encouraged me to complete this endeavor; to the spiritual leaders who blessed me with your teachings, and for helping me to understand God's Word, God's Way and God's Will.

Last, but not least, I'd like to thank all of those persons who have unjustly wronged, despised and/or used me, as well as the perfect strangers who unknowingly blessed me with their generosity, testimonies, and/or acts of kindness during some of the most critical times of my life.

You have *all* played a very instrumental role in helping me to grow stronger and wiser where I needed it most...ultimately leading me to finding an eternal peace within myself, through God's grace and mercy. Thank you and God bless!

Forward

Was an only child for several years;
some actually said that I was spoiled.
Always tried to be and do right,
but to some, I was trouble.

Found out quickly what it meant
to become prey for the vicious ones.
Had to sacrifice my innocence
to undeserving friends of fam.

Was very shy and to myself...
too few friends made me a loner.
Low esteem and indecisiveness
made easy targets for the commoners.

Was a good girl, so I thought,
until one calm, but gloomy night.
Amazing how hiding a hickey
could alter your body and change your life.

Book smart, but the common fell off
when distractions came into play.
Forced to make adult decisions
for the unplanned seed I had to raise.

Married - I always wanted to be,
until the Olympics came into town.
Ten whole years I should've been living,
but instead my spirit was dying.

Born and raised a Georgia peach,
but in my eyes I was nowhere near.
Displeased with my looks...
beautiful – I rarely felt.

Had flings and things and relationships
that I quickly and often let go of –
a defense tactic unconsciously developed
to protect and shield myself.

Developed a swagger like no other...
warm and pleasant was my aurora.
But, no matter how nice I tried to be,
I always managed to gain a hater.

Frequently searched for a break,
but to the System, I was rich.
Laughed and cried at the same time...
'cause my cash flow didn't reflect.

Often wondered why it was
I always got the short end of the stick.
With every attempted shot I would become angry,
until I realized all was meant.

Situations that should have destroyed me
was God's way of making me stronger.
Was inspired to write this book,
in hopes to end the suffering.

I pray my words become a vessel
in which a blessing is delivered.
My hope is that through my testimonies,
a shattered spirit will be lifted.

Thank you for your interest...
may you find peace within these pages.
Your heart may very well touched...
your life may very well be changed.

For I reckon that the sufferings of this present time are not worthy to be compared with the glory which shall be revealed in us.

Romans 8:18 (KJV)

Rounds

ROUND ONE:
DYSFUNKSHUNAL UPBRING'N

A seventies baby, born and raised,
in a small, northwest Georgia town.
Parents were no longer together...
with my mom I was found.
From what I heard – the story goes –
I was the pride and joy of many...
The sweetest little preemie baby...
to my aunts...and to my grands.
Was dressed in the latest fashions –
Neiman Marcus was the label.
Super grades, a gentle demeanor,
a clean room was in my favor.
Obedient and quite respectful,
but found a way to not do right.
To this day, I'm still unclear as to
why a belt was felt each night.
A tomboy...yes, I was –
rode huffy bikes...played street ball.
A heavy hand and a mean tone
made them move or leave me alone.
Had few friends, if at all any,
cause I refused to associate.
Lying tongues and false intentions
only provoked the worst in me.
I can hear the stories now
about my growing up back then.
I would laugh my heart out,
because I'd swear I had a twin.
Can't recall some of the things
that they said I used to do.
Often pondered if I blanked out

when the bad would come through.
Craziness runs in the family;
it's not uncommon to have some issues.
Dysfunctional I was raised,
but the love was always true.
Was called gay once or twice
because my walk was quite reflective...
of the time spent in school hallways,
with my friends – all the fellas.
Didn't bother me at all,
cause it gave me ample opportunity...
To get my pimp on with their boyfriends
(the ones who truly knew me).
But, it's funny how the tables turn –
the very girls who clowned on me...
are now the ones with open closets...
guess the jokes are now on them.
Can't say that I was welcomed...
most people frowned at my existence.
To this day, I've got a cousin
who'd quickly leave whenever I enter.
As I stated, I don't remember
the ill things I may have did...
But, you'd think she'd be over it by now;
after all, we were kids.
Got another cuz, however,
with whom my spirit never liked.
Perhaps it was the gun waved in my face,
or maybe the frequent fights.
He wasn't like another cuz...
I loved that boy with all my heart.
Best break dancer in the A-T-L...
a smart kid...a good sport.
My grandmom was always nice to me...
and her cooking was to die for.

*But, I have yet to figure out how
all that grease could taste so good.
Bingo nights were really fun,
but pitty patt was even better.
Being taught at a young age,
I became queen at winning their nickels.
At home, I was a live-in maid
for my mom – the drill sergeant.
Used to beg to visit my relatives,
so I could be a regular child.
Constant fights I had to watch,
and often run jump in between...
Would always beg her to just be quiet,
because her pain would pain me.
Stubborn, I swear, she was...
the last word she had to get.
Used to cry each and every time
I would hear that dreaded hit.
Was always praying for us to leave,
because I knew I needed her.
Funny, though, how we'd just end up
running into the arms of another.
Sought out ways to remove the drama,
cause love I wasn't really feeling.
Wasn't getting much attention either;
so, to the streets, I quickly fled.
Two hickeys left upon my neck...
hymen stains on the sheets.
Mosquito bites and mother nature were,
of course, the named culprits.
Abused and taken away,
only to become another statistic.
But, I'm stronger and much better –
now – having gone through it.*

**And, ye fathers, provoke not your
children to wrath: but bring
them up in the nurture
and admonition of the Lord.**

Ephesians 5:4 (KJV)

Have you ever looked back over your life – particularly your childhood – and wondered just what that was all about? Have you ever thought back to how one or both of your parents just never seemed to show enough love towards you? Or, how you felt every time you would get into trouble not knowing how or what you did to deserve it? Have you ever wished you could turn back the hands of time to just knock fire out of that bully and/or classmate who insisted on making your day and life miserable? Or, how you would – if you could – go back and change the way you handled certain people and/or situations?

Well...welcome to my world...my thoughts...my reality. I've had all of these feelings and then some. Because, contrary to what some may have thought, growing up was not easy for me.

For 14 years, I was an only child. My cousins all used to say that I was spoiled...that I could ask for and get anything I wanted. That statement may have very well been true – sometimes – when asking of things from my grand-dad or uncle; but, the other 85% of living in my world led me to knowing I was far from being spoiled.

In spite of me having to fight off rowdy cousins and neighborhood bullies, I was always considered [by my elders] to be the well-mannered, sweet, and innocent one. They [my cousins and bullies] were – to me – the mischievous ones...always using me to get things they wanted for themselves...always talking about me or punching on me and going on...always provoking me to have to fight. To look back on it now, one would have thought I was a little Bodie Ali (in the making).

I had always been told that I had heavy hands (that stung like a bee). I think my record back then was 48 and zero. Yep, no one could really touch or hurt me...until that one night my cousin and I were playing... I can vividly remember us frogging each other in the legs (to see who could make the other's leg hurt worse); and, after several back and forths, my cousin must have hit me in the same spot one too many times. I ended up screaming out loudly and laughing hysterically, because he had *finally* managed to hurt me. And, after about two minutes of us laughing, *his* dad (my uncle) burst into the room with a shot gun, cocked it and told my cousin to "get the hell out of the house." Now, my cousin and I were just playing…but, I guess his dad wasn't. My cousin literally had to leave the house. But, me – being the - quote - spoiled one…I got to stay in and continue watching television. Fight over. The only one I technically didn't win; but, that was life on my dad's side.

My dad and mom separated when I was about five months old. He was a borderline alcoholic with a real short temper; so, needless to say, there was a lot of abuse going on…even while my mom was carrying me. I was born a little early weighing in at three pounds, nine ounces…but, apparently as I grew older and bigger, my preemie status was no longer special to my mom.

Living at home with her was almost like living with a military drill sergeant. She was very strict…and was constantly winning awards for being the loudest siren in the neighborhood. That means she was a yeller…about any and every thing she could yell about. But, in addition to the yelling, drill sergeant also had a knack for packing up and relocating – with the quickness.

You see, my mother was the victim of domestic abuse for as long as I can remember. I used to think she liked getting into fights with her boyfriends, because it seemed like that was all she knew. She left my dad because he had a hot temper, and was, as mentioned earlier, very abusive. But, she met another just like him – red boned with an undercover temper. To look at them both, you would have never thought that they would be ones to beat on women…but, I learned very quickly that looks can be quite deceiving.

She was with this second guy for several years…off and on…in between the annual pack up and move sessions. She would leave him…only to go back a couple of months later. I never understood it, as a child…but, now that I've grown up, I've come to realize that some people acquire addictions very early on...her addition was red men.

You would think by me being an honor roll student and an obedient, well-mannered child, that I would be well liked by my mother. But, that – to me – rarely seemed the case. As I mentioned before, I was always getting yelled at. I could, at the age of five, be washing dishes, mopping floors, and dusting every knick knack that she could possibly clutter around the living room...I could keep my room spotless (which I did – and, not because I was made to keep it clean...but, because I've always liked it clean)...but, somehow and in some way, I still managed to get yelled at for something or another. I still managed to do something to earn a whipping for almost every night. And, I still – to this day – cannot understand the whipping received when she was teaching me the symbols shown on playing cards – you know...the spade, club, heart and diamond. I got the club and spade mixed up one time during this *10-minute* session, and got the yellow torn off my behind. Now, someone, please explain that.

Because of those constant whippings and my need to be relieved from being Florence (on *The Jefferson's*), I used to always try to take advantage of the times I got to visit relatives. It was then that I was able to hold my title of 'The Golden Child' by those whom I felt loved me most.

Weekend visits to my grandma's house were always enjoyable. I had my own room and my own bed to sleep in. I could always stay up later than my other cousins. I rarely got chastised – and not because I did no wrong, but mostly because I did no wrong in my grandma's eyes...which, just like my cousins on my dad's side, made a lot of cousins on my mom's side jealous. I found that funny, however, cause all I've ever done to keep from getting into trouble was to do the things I was told and/or asked and/or knew best to do, without any back talk or signs of rebellion. I was hated on because *they* didn't know how to act? Yet, I was considered the *spoiled* one? *Riiiiiight!*

Some would say I had a rather twisted mind, because visiting my aunt and cousin in the rather hood parts of Atlanta was always a nice treat to me. Compared to the small city I was growing up in, Bankhead was considered the big and happening place to be. I always felt like I was somebody special when I went to Atlanta. My cousin and I would hang out all day and most of the night dancing, or playing ball, or sneaking to sit on his mom's car, which she hated. Every kid in the neighborhood knew not to sit on her car...but, somehow, someone always managed to forget. And, well...let's just say, my cousin and I would have a ball counting down the minutes until the front door opened and the cursing began.

My aunt was funny, cool, loveable and direct...and although she could make an enemy in a heartbeat, she was always one of my favorites. It was she that got my ears pierced at a young age. It was she that took me to get me my first hairdo – a Jerry Curl. It was she that allowed me to just be me. My aunt always kept it real to whomever she was talking to, fussing with, cursing out, or looking at...and I loved her for it. But, after those visits were over, it was back home...to the drill sergeant. You know, for years, I thought my mom hated me. And, all I've ever done was love her.

I used to always jump in between her and her boyfriends during their fights, because I would hate to see them hitting her. Sometimes I would succeed...sometimes I just had to sit and cry. I used to just tell her (with tears in my eyes), "*mama, just be quiet...if you stop talking back, he won't hit you no more.*" But, little did that help. She was a very stubborn woman...always having to have the last word.

I never really learned to cook, because I wasn't able to do so while her men friends lived with us. You see, the meals had to be perfect; because, if they weren't, there was sure to be another fight. Yeah, I said "fight". One would think that if I was allowed to cook, she could at least blame it on me, and not have to deal with another day's drama; but, noooo, she had to be the be-all, tell-all, end-of-story one...(I swear I think she liked it).

Now, I'm not judging her...this story is not even about her. I just wanted you to feel me as I paint this picture of what my childhood was like. So, anyway...back to the point I was trying to make. Living at home with my mom was really stressful at times...so stressful that I found myself always trying to find an outlet. Sometimes it was through drawing and/or reading. Sometimes it was through playing with paper dolls in my dollhouse. Sometimes it was just closing my door and daydreaming... wishing that I had a fairy godmother that would come wave her magic wand and blast me away to a better place. No such luck, though. I guess fairytales are just that...fairy tales.

My quest to find that love that I was so desperately craving never ceased. If I couldn't get it at home, I had decided that I was going to get it somewhere. So, like most young girls my age, I found it. It was in a guy that I had met during the frequent visits to the house of my mom's new boyfriend.

Now, this guy I had met was cute, charming...a little on the short side, but fine as he wanted to be. And, I was in love...or, so I thought. This guy was so cunning...and so believable...that he got away with his ultimate plan. I snuck him into the house, after my mom and her boyfriend went to bed, and allowed him to take my innocence. Although he was seven years older than me, he said he loved me, and that he'd always be there for me...and that was all I needed to hear.

Hymen stains on the sheets...two hickeys on my neck. Now, how in the world was I going to hide that? I got up the next morning trying to wash the stained sheets in a small bathroom sink, telling my mom that my menstrual cycle had started. But, as for the hickeys...well, let's just say that I was glad it was in the 80's. The pop-collar shirt trend was great for hiding marks on your neck...or, at least that's what I thought.

The next night, while back at my house, I can recall clearly running down the steps of our town home to get something to drink from the kitchen...and, who pops in from working on the car? My mom's boyfriend. He stopped...did a double-take at my neck, and asked the question (like he didn't already know the answer), "*What are those marks on your neck?*"

Now, y'all, at the age of 13, the best answer I could think of [at that particular moment] was, "*mosquito bites.*" He laughed then turned to walk out of the door, softly saying, "*you better not let your mama see those.*" I immediately fixed my collar back up, and was quite relieved that he didn't say he was going to tell my mom. But, to my surprise, about two minutes later (before I could even finish drinking the grape Kool-Aid I had poured in my cup), she came storming into the house, yelling at the top of her lungs, while forcedly jerking my head from left to right, saying, "*Let me see your neck! Let me see your neck!*"

Uh oh...it was on now.

"*Up to your room!*" she yelled, as she began hitting me with her hands. I ran up the stairs into my room, which she followed shortly after with a belt. She just started swinging...and yelling...and swinging...and yelling...and swinging...and yelling...and, uh, did I say, swinging...and yelling? I was getting hit for so long that I couldn't even remember the words that she was saying. All I remember were the constant snapping sounds from her belt...and me trying to block her next hit with my arms. Well, she finally stopped...and I went to bed...feeling as if I had been stung by 50,000 bees.

The next morning came...and, well...let's just say that after looking at myself in the bathroom mirror, I knew instantly that I wouldn't be going to school *that* day. But, somehow, she thought staying home and washing clothes in our apartment complex's laundry room was a good idea. After looking at my face, again, I began asking myself, "*and just *how am I supposed to leave out of our apartment without getting noticed?"*

And, sure enough, I got noticed.

My best friend (at the time) – a little Madonna wannabe who only went to school when she felt like it – was coming outside to check her mailbox. After seeing me, she ran over to chat, but immediately began screaming, *"What happened to you?! Girl, what happened to you?!"* *"My mama..."* was all I got out of my mouth, and she rushed me into her house to show and tell her mom. Nine. One. One. You know what happened from there. I'd never seen so many cop cars in my life. You would have thought I was being arrested for murdering the president or something. The only thing that I can remember saying was, *"y'all not gonna lock my mama up, are you? I – I – I don't want her to go to jail. She didn't mean it! I swear, she didn't mean it!"*

I was immediately taken to the police station to file a report and have what seemed to be 5,000 pictures taken of me. I hated being there. All I could think about was my mom, and what kind of trouble she was going to be in, coupled with the thought that I was now being labeled as "another one to make the child abuse statistics list."

After what seemed like hours, I was finally taken to a children's shelter owned by the county DFACS office. There were quite a few kids in there...a couple of which I quickly became friends with. It was sad, but comforting at the same time, to know that I wasn't the only one who had gotten abused. Hearing some of their stories, however, actually made me count my blessings. You always tend to think your situation is the worst...until, of course, you hear of someone else's. I realized that my *one* beating was not *that* bad...

...until, of course, the shelter's director, after only two days, told me I had to go to school the following day. *"Like this?!"* I screamed. *"Like that,"* she replied.

Now, here I am walking into my middle school facing eighth grade classmates, who could do nothing but stare, smirk and whisper. By this time, the red whips that were originally on me had now turned into dark purple and black marks, circling around my eyes, neck, chest, arms and legs. Yeah, I didn't just get whipped, y'all...I got 'Whuuuupped!'

But, anyway, I had to listen to all types of remarks...some of which I wanted to fight over...some of which I wanted to cry over. But, all of which made me progressively angry and resentful...towards my mother. The DFACS office told me I couldn't go home for another two years, and awarded temporary custody to my grandmom. It was cool and all. She showered me with the kind of the love that only a grandma could. Aside from living on a dead-end street with very few friends around, and having to go to church *every* Sunday, everything else was gravy...biscuits and gravy...home-made biscuits and gravy, smothered over chicken, with some fried green tomatoes, cheese grits, and scrambled eggs. Umm Ummm. She knew she could cook. But, I swear, if I had to eat chicken one more day, I was going to either die or turn into one.

I truly felt like Forrest Gump as Bubba was describing his Shrimp Boat dream... but instead of shrimp, I was having chicken...fried chicken, baked chicken, boiled chicken, broiled chicken, roasted chicken, barbeque chicken, chicken and gravy, chicken pot pie, chicken lasagna, chicken and dumplings, chicken casserole, chicken salad, chicken soup, chicken livers, chicken gizzards...we even had chicken hot dogs and chicken bologna. And, yes...just like it was painful for you to read all of that, it was equally as painful eating it...every day.

But, I gotta give it to her...on the days she decided to grant my wish of making something other than chicken, her homemade pizzas, fried pork chops, macaroni and cheese and iron skillet-baked cornbread and dressing, washed down with about five glasses of her sweet tea...well, that was like heaven...on any given day. She was, indeed, an awesome cook.

During the two years I lived with my grandma, my father passed away in a house fire. Now I wasn't really that close to my father (as I only got to see him during summer and winter vacations); but, hearing the story and seeing him (along with two of my uncles and one of their girlfriend's) on the news all day and night [for three days straight] was extremely hard for me. I may have been 15 years old; but, I cried like a baby each and every time I saw their faces show up on the screen. How could not one person (out of four people) survive a house fire?

It was rumored that my dad was messing around with a white lady...a married white lady. It was also rumored that three gunshots and a woman's scream was heard shortly before the house went up in flames. But, let the detectives tell it (or not tell it), their deaths was from an old kerosene heater that malfunctioned...yet, everyone was in separate rooms throughout a 2,800-square foot house. Right. That's what I said.

Now, there was no question that my dad had made quite a few enemies over his lifetime. No one could touch him, though. He was feared by many and known by most as the 'crazy one that you didn't want to mess with'. Underneath his fearless and high tempered shield, he was actually a pretty nice guy, though. It was just advised that you always stay in your place, and don't ever take his kindness as a sign of weakness. He was always on guard, even while drunk, and would cut a negro [or any man] in a heartbeat.

Many say that I carry the same or similar characteristics. But, luckily for whomever (and me, for that matter), I have yet to be coerced and/or placed into a situation deep enough to make me want to live out my father's legacy.

About a month after my father's death, my grandfather was admitted into the hospital. He had suffered with diabetes for many years; but, after learning of my father's death, he almost immediately stopped eating and taking care of himself. You see, my father was his only child.

I had never heard anyone talking out of their mind before; but, on that day, I had an experience. I saw death in my grandfather's face. I heard death in his voice. A week later, I was headed to his funeral. That was the first time I had ever kissed a dead person in a casket. But, you have to understand, I LOVED my grand-dad. He was one of the sweetest men I had ever known…the only man, aside from my dad's sister's husband, who I could look up to…the only one who took me fishing and to the parks…bought me ice cream and candy every day…and gave me money whenever I asked…the only man I had truly loved and respected. Now, if I was spoiled, I was spoiled by him – definitely. But, that ended, shortly following my 15th birthday.

After the two years of living with my grandmother were up, I went back to living with my mom. No more 'whuuppins', but the yelling never stopped. I found it funny how I, the one who never talked back, never looked at her sideways, never jumped bad in her face, never did or said anything disrespectful to or towards her, could be hated so much. Perhaps she saw my father every time she looked at me. Perhaps she had insecurities with my near grown look. I don't know what it was. And, honestly, I still don't.

But, I was glad to finally have a little sister come along. The first live birth I had gotten to witness (because her father didn't want to be in the room). She was cute, and though I didn't realize it then, she actually took a lot of pressure off of me.

My mom didn't really have time to worry about what was going on with me any longer. Her focus shifted solely on her 'new little baby girl' and that tattle tale of a man whom you would have thought was a dark skinned 'Prince Charming' or somebody. I didn't like him – not one bit. Perhaps it was because his gentle and seemingly romantic shield was finally unveiled to show the snake in sheep's clothing that he really was. No more T-bone steaks, waffles and cheese eggs in the morning. Now, we got fights, and head banging. Now we got crack, and cocaine smoking. Now we got accusations, guns and bullets…and me yelling, *"you're lucky you're in this [cop] car, cause I would kill your ass...I swear I would!"* Ummm, hmmm...that was the first time I had ever cursed at a grown up...but, I didn't know. You see, I thought my mom was dead. All I heard was loud arguing, a gunshot and then there was total silence. Not even my sister (who was in the room with them) made a sound. But, love is a funny thing. After all the talks about not seeing him again, I guess my sister being his child prevented that from happening. My mom...as always...went back.

That was cool with me, though. I stopped stressing over her mess. She liked it, she got it. Besides, with little attention on me, I was able to continue 'finding myself.'

I Wish I Was A Butterfly

I wish I was a butterfly...
so I could fly far away...
to a place where people love me...
to a place I'd want to stay.

I wish I was a butterfly...
so beautiful it would be...
to be admired for the good,
to have no faults found in me.

I wish I was a butterfly...
on a pretty summer day...
able to smell my favorite flower...
to ease or take my pain away.

I wish I was a butterfly...
able to withstand the rain that falls....
No worries to get me down,
nobody to have to call.

I wish I was a butterfly...
able to live my life in harmony...
No more tears to have to wipe...
what a sweet joy that would be...

I wish I was a butterfly...
looking God in the eye.
to thank Him for rescuing me...
to thank Him for saving my life.

Recoil...

You know they always say, God has a way of taking us through things to make us stronger, and to eventually show us that there is a rainbow after each storm. I, at the time, didn't know just how He was blessing me...but, now, looking back on everything, I see the big picture.

I grew up tom-boyish, fighting off rowdy boys. I grew up watching the abuse my mom sometimes caused and constantly took. I grew up with people not liking me. I grew up having to defend my name and having to make a 'life' for myself.

Unknowingly, though, I was being strengthened...trained...prepared. Not only was I gaining courage to stand up for myself, I was also seeing the types of things that I knew I didn't want to deal with when I got older. But, more importantly, I was seeing how and what I didn't want to be...realizing that I wanted to be nothing like those around me.

That was the beginning of His ministry to me.

My prayers and cries were often...and though I had always heard of God, I had not really taken the time to get to know Him. One thing I did learn, however, while going to church every Sunday with my grandma, was that if I ever needed help, God would be the best one to call.

During my struggles as a child to fit in, to be accepted, to be loved...I often questioned my value...my worth. I was always trying to do things that I knew would please those around me, simply because I thought that would make them like me...love me. Not knowing that throughout every trial and situation, I already had love all around me, and it wasn't in the people with whom I was trying to please.

I didn't have to be a people pleaser. I didn't have to do things that I knew were wrong, just to keep friends and family happy with me. All I had to do was the right thing...and God would take care of the rest.

There were several times when my mom would pack up and leave her abusive boyfriends. During those times, I felt my prayers were being answered. But, every time she went back, I found myself immediately questioning God and what I thought were His decisions. Sometimes I even became angry. Why was He forcing my mom to deal with these abusive men? Why wasn't He moving us to a better life? Why was He cursing us? Did He not love us? Did we do something wrong?

That was the beginning of Him speaking to me.

It wasn't that we were doing anything wrong...it was Him trying to reach out to us...to try to get us to see that His love was greater than every body else's.

I began realizing (from hearing and watching my mom and her boyfriends during their feuds) that a man hitting on you doesn't mean that he loves you. As a matter of fact, it meant the complete opposite. Love is not controlling. Love is not abusive. Love is not demanding. It is not blasphemy, nor hatred. Love is not jealous or inpatient. Love is Love. God is love. And, although I didn't know this then, knowing it now makes all the difference. Just knowing who and what type of spirit God is makes me appreciate and hold close the relationship that I've developed with him.

God is not controlling or demanding; as a matter of fact, He gives you choices, and also gives you free will to select which choice and/or path you would like to take. God is not abusive or filled with hate; He is, instead, gentle and comforting to His children...to those who love Him...to those who diligently seek Him. God *is* jealous, however...but, only HE has that right to be. Besides, it was HE that first knew us...HE that first made us...HE that first loved us...HE that will always love us, despite and/or regardless of our faults and failures. No man, no woman, no child, animal or thing could ever love us the way God does.

The thing I realized while growing up was that, in every situation, I always had a hand covering me...shielding me...loving me. Yeah, there were things I went through. Yeah, there were things I had seen. There were even things I had heard. But, none of them even came close to the things I was made to feel.

Despite my situations, the negative thoughts, the lack of love, the betrayals, the deaths...my God was always there...showing me how to think for myself and look out for myself...as well as how to handle persons who promoted and/or caused strife in my life.

Now, the Bible teaches us that we should love everyone...and, I do. But, I have very little respect for some persons...

...Like parents who take advantage of their childrens' weaknesses...who prey on their innocence...who fail to protect and/or provide for their children...who don't believe in their worth...who unnecessarily ridicule and degrade their children...and who try to live their unfulfilled lives vicariously through their children. Parents, you should help your children to be the best that they can be. Never compare them to other children, for each is his own individual. Love them for who they are. Teach them the ways in which they should go...and they will, in turn, appreciate, respect and value you, as a parent, more that you can possibly imagine.

And for those who have kids acting or lashing out, my only advice to you is 'Get to the bottom of it.' Kids can say a lot of things (verbally or through expressions) to let you know that something is going on with them...all you have to do is take the time to ask and talk with them. Some are in need of attention...some are in need of knowing that someone cares about them and their wellbeing...some are in need of knowing that they are supported and valued...some may be dealing with thoughts and/or situations they don't understand...and, all are in need of knowing that you love them. So, take time...make time...for your children. After all, it was *you* that brought them here, not they, themselves.

And, for you kids who dishonor, disobey and/or disrespect your parents...you should honestly think twice about your actions. It is written and confirmed that those who dishonor their parents displease God. And, I don't know about you...but, out of all of the people in the world with whom I could have as an enemy, I surely don't want God – the maker of heaven and earth, the creator of man and woman and every living thing that exists on the earth today, the all-powerful and all knowing, the one who blesses me [and you] every day with breath and a sane mind, the one who could ultimately take my [and your] life at any given moment in time – to find me [or you] guilty of mistreating my [or your] parents. And, especially not the parents that He placed together to make me [and you]...to take care of me [and you]...and to love me [and you].

Now, I'm not saying that all parents are good parents, as all fall short of the glory; but, what I am saying is that they all deserve respect and appreciation. Parents were used by God as a means to populate the world with children who can carry out His mission. And, although they may accomplish the planting of the seeds, some parents have difficulty nurturing those seeds. This would be because parents are people who, too, can easily be distracted, confused, misled, and/or addicted to damaging behaviors. But, to be blessed with a parent or parents that truly do 'try' to care for and love you the best that they know how...my only advice is that you watch yourself with regards to how you treat them.

They are still in your life for a reason. God still has them there...blessing you, in one way or another. Be thankful, because what you don't see or realize is that God is working. And, you, dishonoring or disrespecting your parents could be the very thing that stops His would-have-been-soul-prospering plan and/or direction for your own life. And, although it may not happen immediately, trust me when I say that God has a way of showing you your faults, and His chastisement is nothing like that of which your parents could or would ever give. He is, again, all powerful...you can be one day enjoying the magnificence of his grace, and the next day struck with bad health, lack of prosperity, disobedient and unruly kids yourself, or even death. He is not to be tempted. And, I definitely wouldn't anger him enough to have His wrath come upon you.

There are other and much better ways to deal with parents 'who just don't understand'. Those you just don't like. Those you feel treat you unfairly or wrong. If they're not trying to literally kill you, your best option (until you are old enough to leave or live on your own) is to listen to their advice, recognize what *you* are doing wrong and accept the disciplinary actions that are resulting from those doings; and, don't dare open your mouth to talk back in a disrespectful tone or manner...but, most of all, act like the child God made you to be. Thought: If God was the one disciplining you, would you treat and/or disrespect Him in the same manner in which you are treating/disrespecting your mom or dad? Be careful. Be very, very careful.

I know this may sound a little cliché, but, think about it. You're younger... they're older. You're just beginning to experience what life is all about; whereas, your parents (and other elders) have already gone through the things you're trying to go through.

As a child I had to learn that just because I *thought* something was right or best, it didn't always mean that it was. In fact, now that I am an adult, looking back over my childish ways of thinking, I realized that my mom and other elders were actually telling me the truth. They would always say, "*we've been there, done that, and are trying to keep you from going down that same road.*"

I have found myself saying those exact same words to my own children. And, trust me when I say, even though generations have been known to change, life hasn't. It was written thousands of years ago and has been proven every generation since then that there's nothing new under the sun...what goes around will come back around...what goes up must come back down.

Young folk, you probably don't know me from a hole in your sock; but, trust me when I say, you should heed the advice that your elders give. It may very well be God (speaking through them) in efforts to keep you from going down a path that would only prove destructive to His plan for you and/or your life.

As a youngster, I had to learn to cope and move on. I realized that although I was beaten for having sex early, was seemingly placed second to my mom's boyfriends, was often used as a housemaid, and daily spoken to as if I was a private first class, my mom still loved me. She had a very funny way of showing it...but, God still used her to do the things she did, so that I can – ultimately – turn out to be the person I am today. She was my first mentor...my first guide...my first role model. God used her, and is still using her to mold and shape me.

Of course, I see things in my mom that I don't like...that I hope to not become...that I pray she is delivered from. But, I'm not her creator. I have not a heaven or hell to place her in, and I have no business at all trying to play God in her life.
What I [and you] can do, however, is pray and trust that God will make your home life better. In one way or another, as long as you remain faithful, He will, indeed, answer your prayers.

Moving on, another type of person that I have very little respect for would include men [or women] who get their rocks off by physically abusing their mates. It truly pains me to know that a person would want to be in control so much that they would do it at the expense of another person's wellbeing. I have deep sorrow for the victims who remain in these types of relationships – out of fear or confusion; and, I pray that all are awakened and delivered from this madness before it is too late.

Satan has succeeded in causing havoc in so many lives that he has been able to destroy relationships by stealing what little joy and peace they could have had. For this reason alone, I am extremely thankful for the opportunity to get to know God on such a personal level.

I've been blessed by what I was able to see and learn from my childhood, as every experience, along with God's words and presence in my life, has shaped and/or reshaped my way of thinking:

1) I have learned to watch what I say to people, as well as how I say it; because, just like me, everyone has a battle of some sort (if not many) that they're fighting. So, who am I to add to their burdens? And, why would or should I?

2) I have learned to not say anything, if I don't have anything *nice* to say. I know what it feels like to have others try and cut you down, especially when it doesn't make sense and is rarely necessary. It's so easy for us to do or say something hurtful to someone; so, why not challenge ourselves to do the harder task, which is really not that hard at all – to just be nice to someone... Smile. Think of and share a compliment instead of an insult. Bring joy to someone's life. You never know...you may be the blessing that God is trying to use to save that person's life.

3) I have learned that fighting a man (or having relations with a violent and hot-tempered man) is not for me. If God ain't beating on me, why on earth would I let a man who has not even a tenth of the love that God has for me put his hands on me? As mentioned earlier, trying to manipulate someone through physical force is wrong. And, although this is still a very common dilemma in our communities, I still pray for our sisters (and brothers) who find themselves going through this type of torment daily. Stay strong, and listen for God's voice. You will know what to do and when. Note: Hot grits and an iron skillet – I've heard – works wonders, too.

4) I have also learned to not put all of my trust into those who I *think* have my best interest in mind. People are peculiar, habitual and fair-weather creatures. You do or say one wrong thing, and they're out of your life...or, spitefully trying to use you...or, talking behind your back...or, trying to do whatever they can to negatively provoke your emotions. I have found that when others let you down or speak negatively of you, God is always there to lift you up and give you peace.

5) I have learned what not sparing the rod means (whether it is deserved or not). Parents have a hard job trying to raise their children to do and be right...to not make life-altering mistakes...to not be lazy and careless, but instead to be compelled to make a positive difference in the world. It really isn't easy...being a parent. And, for this reason, I have learned to appreciate the value that they bring, as well as the sacrifices that many make just to make sure their children are fed, clothed, and sheltered.

6) And, through it all, I have also learned that I never wanted to be like my mom...I wanted to be better. As my first role model, I got to see – first hand – what to do or what not to do, with regards to building relationships with your children, family or companions. I also learned that I, me, personally, wanted to excel beyond my comfort level...to have the things I wanted in life – materialistically, emotionally and spiritually.

I have learned that there are a lot of situations in which we may go through as a child and/or young adult (and even through our adulthood); but, the one thing we should always keep in the forefront of our minds is the fact that through it all, God is always there.

ROUND TWO:
WRONG'D

To the incest perpetrators, molesters,
pedophiles and rapists...
Thank you for the anguish
you've softly brought upon me.
My memory runs deep like a
bad dream that keeps replaying.
From the ripe age of four,
I've always been the chosen victim.
The selfishness of your actions
was like pure torture to me.
Lost my childhood to a man...
a so-called friend of the family.
Often tried to reveal this pain,
but love for them outweighed me.
So, I stayed quiet, often angered,
that I had to alone deal with this.
Roughened hands, a dirty mind,
perversion beyond all compare.
From childhood to adulthood,
my screams he deeply buried.
Latch key kid from the very beginning;
she trusted God - obviously.
Never told about that long walk home...
the first time for my life I feared.

Used to think I was rather pretty,
but never knew I was the charm.
The devil truly has a way of
bringing the worst out of some.
The ones you trusted are now the ones
you're scared to stay alone with.
Would beg and plead to visit family,
cause I hated being around him.
Recall telling of this problem,
but it got shunned like I knew not.
Could have really killed me then,
cause in my world, I'd already died.
There were perks, but the jealous rages
were off the charts in my book.
The only way I learned to drive
was to not get my boyfriends hooked.
Never went to my prom and
was never allowed to stay out late...
Still don't understand why at the age of 20
my curfew was midnight.
Was losing weight, having stomach issues,
crying to sleep every evening.
But, saving my mama was the goal,
for I needed her to keep on living.
There were many days and many ways
that I would think about his death.
Thought I loved him like a dad,
until I was forced upon his wrath.

Prayed on my knees every night,
cause my sanity was at risk.
The threats and constant approaches
were now causing resentment.
Contemplated, premeditated,
often thought of horrific ways
that I could kill him, truly hurt him...
just wanted him far away from me.
Prayed and cried, cried and prayed,
until that day I was finally rescued.
Gone at the age of 20...
my paternal aunt, I owe it all to.
Life has a funny way of turning
the tables and changing the channels.
Could have been dead or behind bars;
but, free I was found.
Able to move on with my life,
and although the struggles still do linger...
God is faithful in His Word...
no longer can they harm or hurt me.
May have taken longer than I'd wished,
but they reaped what they sewed.
The suffering that they caused me,
God sent back seven folds.
Bet they wished they hadn't done it...
for their lives they might still have.
Seen two of them laid to rest,
and not one tear did I shed.

Forgiven, yes I have...
but the memories are far from being gone.
I've got peace, though – finally,
because I'm not suffering any more.

**As for me, I will call upon God;
and the Lord shall save me.**

Psalm 55:16 (KJV)

Statistics[1]:

- 1 in 6 women will be sexually assaulted over their lifetime.
- 34% of victims of sexual assault and rape are under age 12.
- 55% of sexual assaults take place in or near the victim's home.
- Almost 3/4 of all rapes are committed by someone known to the victim.
- 2 out of 3 sexual assaults never get reported to the police.
- Only 4% of rapists will ever spend a day in jail.

1 – As reported by the Rape, Abuse & Incest National Network, 2016

This may very well be one of the hardest chapters in this book for me to write. The pain and anguish that's still buried deep within me seems to resurface every time I even think about my past. But, I pray that God will guide my mind and fingers as I begin to reveal this pain to you.

While scanning and searching my memory for anything that might have happened in my early childhood, the first and only thing I can remember (stemming back to the age of four) was me lying on my bed playing with my genitals [as I was often taught to do]. For him, it was a game of some sort. I was supposed to see if I could make myself feel good. And, then I was supposed to see if *he* could make me feel good.

Feel good?

What that was to a four-year-old child, I have no idea. What that is to me now...a reason to burn someone alive.

All my life, or through early adulthood at least, I've had to deal with twisted and perverse minds. Molestation, incest, and rape were all a reality to me. Growing up, I knew when the acts were wrong. Anytime we had to sneak or only do something when someone else wasn't around, that, to me, spelled wrong.
And fearing for my life was even more wrong.

I can recall this older boy, or bully, who used to watch me walk home from school every day. He knew my every route. He knew what time I left for school. He knew what time I made it home. He knew what time my mom would get in from work. I was all of about six or seven.
On this day, he approached me, and coerced me into following him behind an abandoned building (near my school). He said he had something to show me...and because I had often seen him around, I just thought he was being friendly. But that all changed as soon as we turned that corner. He grabbed me – violently – shaking me, and trying to force me to take my clothes off. He was a big boy.

I can distinctly hear his voice firmly stating that I "*better not scream...that I better let him do it...that I better not tell nobody, or else he was going to kill me.*" I was scared. I was terrified. But, just as he was about to commence to forcing himself inside of me, I was moved to draw back to my Bodie Ali training. I fought. I kicked. I punched. I threw rocks... all while trying to put my clothes back on. And then, I ran. "Run, Forrest, Run!" That could have been me on that day.

I ran all the way home, hoping and praying that he wasn't following me... that he wasn't going to break into my house before my mama got home.

The phone just so happened to ring as soon as I got my key into the door. It was my mom screaming to the top of her lungs, asking why I hadn't called her, yet (not knowing I was *just* getting home). My excuse for being over 30 minutes late was because all of my bows fell out of my head, and I had to keep picking them up...and then, my shoestrings kept coming untied... Now, y'all, again, I was only six or seven years old...so, of course, the excuses wouldn't make sense.

There were a few occasions after that in which I would see the bully boy; he always had this mean look...and always whispered crap like he 'was gonna get me'. But, fortunately, he never approached or messed with me again.

Another memory takes me to a time in which I told my mom of her boyfriend coming into my room (around the age of 10 or 11) to fondle me. Her response was that "he said" he was putting the covers over me, because it was a little chilly in the house. I found it funny how putting the covers over me involved his hands creeping between my legs. I found it even more funny, however, how he had come to do something that was already done. My covers were already over me.

He was quite upset at my mentioning of that little act to my mom...so upset that he made a point to get his threat out the next day. He said he would kill her and me, if I ever told again; and, because of all the fighting that they used to do, I actually believed him. So, I just dealt with it...silently...from that point forward.

But, I was becoming tired. Tired of him noticing my body. Tired of me being made to notice his. I used to always say, "*you have a grown, fully developed, able-to-sex-you-in-any-way-you-want-to-be-sexed woman in the other room. So, why you gotta mess with me?*"

I used to hate to see them argue and fight; but, I must admit that I was always glad when it was pack up and dip time. That always meant a 'break' for me. Or, better yet, it meant freedom. Freedom from the anguish that was often provoked. Freedom from the mental and physical turmoil that would put undue pressure on my spirit. But, unfortunately, that freedom was only temporary.

For some reason or another, she always managed to go back. And, every time she did, the advances would resume and increase. It seemed the older I would become, the more things were being introduced to me. Pornography tapes were being watched. Perverse artwork was drawn, carved and/or painted, and freely left lying around the house. Sex was as common as *Sesame Street*. I was becoming more adept to learning matters relating to sex and sexuality, more so than the things I needed to learn and retain for school, etc. For years, I was being subjected to things I should not have been. And, for years, I just wished I could have a normal childhood.

My outlet – in my early teens – became boys. I stopped playing with my paper dolls. I stopped drawing and reading. I stopped everything that I thought I used to find contentment in, because I was no longer content. I figured if I had to let someone touch me, it might as well be someone with whom I wanted to touch me. So, I gave in.

During my mom's breakup with that boyfriend and her immediate move to the next one, I began having sex, to see what it actually felt like...to see just what it was that made men feel like they just had to take the innocence of young girls. I had to see. But, that first time...I saw nothing. I felt nothing...but, pain.

Her next boyfriend exposed my secret by revealing the fact that I had hickeys on my neck. After having the knowledge that I was no longer a virgin, I guess he felt it would be cool to get in on a piece of the action, too. I never would have thought he would have attempted to do such a thing...but, on the nights my mom was in the hospital after giving birth to my sister, the unthinkable was happening.

Fellatio and penetration...on the side of the road...in the house...on the side of the road again. I hated this. I hated being preyed upon. I hated that I was the only one going through this. What did I do to ever deserve this? Why was God allowing these men to use and abuse me in this way? When was the pain going to stop? Was the pain ever going to stop?

I prayed that he would leave me alone. And, to my surprise, he did. He never approached me again after my mom came home with my sister. But, I never forgot. He thought teaching me how to drive a manual-shift car would keep me quiet. It did for a year. But, after he shot my mom, and she took him back, I tried my best to keep him away from us. I told my aunts and uncle about what he had done to me, and they immediately took me to the police station to file a report. Little good that did. Apparently, because it took me over a year to report it, and because I had had sex with other guys since then, my report was null and void. I could no longer prove that he performed those acts, so my accusations were not enough to convict him. My word wasn't good enough?

Pain...again.

While he and my mom were in and out of separation mode, I wrote a letter to my so-called daddy figure (the first molester), explaining that my mom's ex-boyfriend had shot her, explaining how he tried to mess with me, and how I didn't want my mama to have a chance to take him back. Less than two months later, this man had moved back from Alabama to Georgia and was living with us...again.

Everything was good at first. He and my mom seemed happy. No attempts to touch or mess with me. I thought he was a reformed man...a better man.

Not hardly.
This time it was worse. Cause, he, too, knew that I was no longer a virgin. Heck, I had had a child by that time. If that didn't mean I was no longer a virgin, I don't know what did. But, regardless, I was seventeen...and hating it. Hating that I ever contacted him. Hating that I was being forced. Hating that I had no one to turn to...to talk to.

The arguments and fights with my mom resumed. And, all over again, my hatred for this man resurfaced.

Like the other, the only way I learned to drive was to [while making some unnecessary trip to the store, etc.] have sex with him. The only way I could get some spending change was to have sex with him. The only way to keep him in a decent mood was to have sex with him. Never could I exercise alone...cause apparently, there were perks in 'helping' me stay fit. Never was I left alone...sex toys had to be explored and used, and a variety of positions had to be tried out. I learned the various ways of achieving orgasms, although all were faked [just so that he would get off of me].

Some would say I got something good out of it, as I learned how to please a man...but, to me, none of it was good. I hated it. And, I hated him.

He used to always say I was what he was looking for in a wife, and that we were going to go off one day and get married. I used to say, *"you're the same age as my daddy...why would I marry you?"* He'd always get mad and say I hurt his feelings...but, why his sick mind couldn't see that marrying him was nowhere near feasible, I don't know. All I do know is that I used to always wish my dad was still living. I wanted someone to call. Someone who would handle this situation and/or get rid of this man. I needed some "see tho, what it is tho" action.

It had gotten so bad with this guy that any young man I even dared think about talking to, being with, or going out with, the answer was always, "No," or "he ain't right for you," or "all he wants is to get between your legs." And, every time, I used to wonder just why he couldn't put himself into those categories. Did he not know that he wasn't right for me either?

I often looked to my mom for help, cause I truly felt like if anyone should stop me from dating, it should be her. After practically begging her, she finally pleaded my case and was able to persuade him to let me go on one date. After all, I was 20 years old.

So, I went...but, I had to be back by midnight.

Did I say I was 20? With a baby already? So, why a curfew of midnight? If I hadn't made any more babies in four years, I don't think it would have been in the plans to make one that night.

But anyway, I came home about five minutes past my midnight curfew, and, literally had to hear about it for the next few days. It seemed that the old man was furious...talking about he didn't like the fact that I was giving his stuff away.
His stuff?

Did I say I hated him?

I hated him. So much that I began thinking of ways in which I could get rid of him. I called my thug of an ex-boyfriend...but, then chickened out. Knowing of an existing warrant, I called the police to inform them that he was hiding out at our house...only to find that my mom succeeded in hiding him in her closet when the police came. I tried reading books, etc. to see which poisons could kill him with the least suspicion. I walked around police supply stores to see which devices I could use to blow his car up and not get found out and/or convicted. I cried...every night.

But, one night, when all else was leading to a dead end, I prayed... begging God to help me, because I knew it was only a matter of time. I was either going to kill him and end up behind bars for the rest of my and my son's life; or, he was going to kill me, my son, my mom, and my sister, because I revealed his dirty secret. I needed an outlet. I had lost over 15 pounds. I began having stomach ailments and migraines. I began feeling hopeless...like I was stuck in this hell hole for the rest of my life.

I needed an outlet. And, I needed it soon.

God answered my prayer about two weeks later. My father's sister called me one day, and I could no longer hold it in. The next day, she and my uncle came down and picked me and my son up. I was gone. I was finally gone.

Gone from the constant arguments and fights. Gone from the possessive and obsessive nutcase that was preventing me from doing the things a young woman my age should have been able to do. Gone from the turmoil and the upset stomachs caused by unwanted advances and acts that I was made to perform. Gone. Promising myself that I would never, ever allow anyone to take advantage of me and/or my sexuality again. Gone. Finally gone.

I Despise You

From as early as I can remember, you have touched me.
Used to always call me your daughter, but you wronged me.
Had to deal with your advances, cause you loved me?
A sick pervasion in your mind...and you can't see...

That I despise the man you are, yes I despise you.
For all the things you've done to me, I despise you.
For all the ways you've made me suffer, I despise you.
For all the shame you've brought upon me, I despise you.

I wished my daddy was still living, cause he'd kill you.
And, if you keep on touching me, he's gonna come through.
You look at me with that smurk, as if you don't believe.
Keep on trying, keep on risking, you'll soon see.

My body's hurting, tears are flowing...I despise you.
Trying to think of something bad, cause, I despise you.
Every night I pray you'd flee...I despise you.
Close my eyes and hope for death...cause I despise you.

Got my mama on your side, cause she can't see.
Push all my boyfriends away so you could have me?
You wouldn't do this to your daughters, but you choose me?
A lot of nerve...coward man...hope you hear me.

You better pray I find a break, cause I despise you.
You better hope God gives me strength...cause I despise you.
I hope and pray I can forgive...I despise you.
No other words I can say, but these stand true...

For all the pain and the anguish...I Despise You.

**"And the Lord, he it is that doth go
before thee; he will be with thee, he
will not fail thee, neither forsake thee:
fear not, neither be dismayed."**

Deuteronomy 31:8 (KJV)

Recoil...

I cannot begin to tell you how alone I felt. Not being able to tell anyone. Always being made to keep silent...and to just deal with it. I cannot begin to tell you how often I felt there was no God. Besides, how could He allow those men to continue causing me grief.

I cannot begin to tell you how often I regretted my real father having died when I was 15. I truly felt if he was living, he would have handled the situations for me. I cannot begin to tell you how much I resented my mother for not believing in me...for subjecting me...for not protecting me. After all, most of my dealings were with *her* boyfriends.

I cannot begin to tell you how much I, after years of being 'gone', still harbored hatred in my heart. Shying away from those very men in my adult years for fear of what I might say or do. I cannot begin to tell you how after two of the men passed away, not one single tear was shed as an expression of sorrow. I can't say I was overjoyed that they had died; but, I was relieved to know that they could no longer bother me.

I cannot begin to tell you how -- even though I've forgiven, my mind, body and spirit have yet to forget. It is still so very easy for me to relive each and every moment whenever the thoughts resurface.

I cannot begin to tell you just why it is my thoughts and actions towards men do not depict my resentfulness of my past...but, what I can tell you is that if it wasn't for the grace of God, I don't think I would be here writing this book today.

For those of you who have never had to go through the agony of unwanted sexual advances, take a moment to thank God right now. Then, pray that he continues to shield you for the rest of your years. You have been blessed.

For those of you who *are* like me, however, having had all types of unwanted sexual advances, take comfort in the fact that you, too, are blessed. It may not feel like it. It my not sound like it. It may not even look like it. But, one thing I've learned is that just when you think God isn't listening...just when you think God is nowhere around...just when you think it is useless to praise Him in the midst, He shows up...just in time...to prove to you just why He's God.

From the teachings at the age of four, to the incident with the big bully boy, to the last encounter before I left my mother's home, the road has always been rocky. Never knowing who or which moment was going to be used as a 'torture Bodie' moment. Never knowing if God was going to send His wrath in the middle of the act, or if He was going to allow it through completion. Never knowing just when I would proclaim I'd had enough, and release the Bodie war fighter who I knew had been buried deep all of my life.

With no one to tell, and nowhere to go, what do you do? When no one will listen...when no one will believe you, what do you do? When you know you'll be the one blamed because your body is rather tempting, what do you do? When you know you'll be looked at as the one who provoked it, what do you do? When you know you'll be added to that awful statistics list, what do you do? What *do* you do?

I cried. Silently. Until I couldn't cry any more.

After that, I fell to my knees and began praying to God. I begged. I pleaded. I warned, '*God, please save me...or forgive me for whatever it is I might do wrong in your sight.*'

All I knew is that if I got touched one more time. If I got kissed with cigarette breath one more time. If I got told I was going to be someone's wife one more time. If I got made to have sex one more time. If I saw the perverseness in their eyes one more time. If I got told I was loved one more time...that was going to be it.

Fortunately (and unfortunately), that one more time didn't end when I wished it would. Had I not waited on the Lord to save me, there's no telling where I would be. I could imagine, however, being behind a row of steel bars and barbwire, or perhaps drugged up in somebody's psychiatric ward, or perhaps even nicely pushing six feet of dirt somewhere. All of those scenarios would mean that my mission – in some way – failed. But, thank God, I'm still here, in the comforts of my own home, expressing myself to you.

For those young girls who are still struggling with the daily attempts to attack your innocence, call on God. For those of you who have tried to tell, but your stories have seemingly fallen on deaf ears, call on God. For those women who are being stalked and/or forced to live their lives in fear, call on God. For those girls who have that funny suspicion that you're being watched, call on God. Pray. But, most of all, have FAITH that God will come through for you. That He will protect you. That He will save you. After all, you are His child. He made you. And, surely, if He loved you enough to make you, He wouldn't lead you where His grace couldn't follow, protect and/or deliver you.

For those of you who don't yet know God...who have never tried God...who have yet to experience the goodness that knowing Him can bring, I ask you to right now take a moment to start that talk. To take that walk. He's everywhere. If you have to meet Him in the bathroom, that's fine. If you have to meet Him in the car, that's fine. If you have to meet Him in your closet, that's fine, too. He doesn't care where you go to meet Him...just meet Him. Call on Him. He's waiting.

Out of all the men who I felt wronged me, never would I ever think or say again, that one of them was God. As mentioned before, I often wondered where God was when I needed Him most...but, that old faithful saying of "God not being there when you want Him, but always being there when you need Him" proved true.

What I had to learn is that there will always be times and there will always be things that God allows us to go through and/or experience; but, this is what helps to make us soldiers [for Him]. If we never go through anything, we will never know what it feels like to conquer. If we never go through anything, we will never have a reason to praise Him when it's all over. If we never go through anything, we will never be capable of witnessing to others about the greatness of God's mercy.

I am a living testimony. I am a survivor. Praise be to God.

Another thing I took note of, after my ordeals with the men who wronged me, is that whosoever shall harm or make a child of God call out to Him, that person or persons will indeed be made to pay for their wrongful actions.

Now, it may have taken years after the ordeals had ceased, but trust me when I say that the perpetuators received their payback for all of the pain and anguish that they caused me. For every tear I shed, for every bit of pain I felt, God repaid them. First, it was through addictions...then, it was through failing health...and, finally, it was through death. Now, again, I'm not saying that death was what I wished (at the times of their death); but, what I am saying is that God doesn't like ugly...and, what goes around comes back around. The same pain you cause on someone else will be the same pain that will come back onto you. 2 Thessalonians 1:6 says, "God is just: He will pay back trouble for those who trouble you."

Now, as a young woman, even through today, I have never thought of myself as being breathtakingly beautiful or finer than fine wine...nor have I ever thought that I would be targeted as the object of desire for most men. But, I'm glad that I was able to hang on...and keep the faith. It was that faith God used to guide me, to see me through, and to deliver me.

One of the biggest lessons I had to learn from everything that I went through was that I shouldn't try to 'understand' that of which I cannot; but, instead, I should concentrate and focus more on the miracle that's going to take place in the morning. There is a reason for everything that we go through. Whether it is to teach us or to strengthen us or to prepare us...there is still a reason.

My situations, I believe, were meant to serve as experience. Experience that I lived through and can now share with others as just one of my many testimonies. Though I hated every advance made towards me then, I'm thankful now, for each and every encounter, as they made me stronger. Stronger as a victimized young girl. Stronger as an abused adolescent. Stronger as a targeted young woman.

I have had to learn [the hard way] to never trust an innocent look...to never trust that all who appear to like or love you and your children really do...to never trust that everyone who talks a good game will have your best interest in mind. There are quite a few vultures out there whose sole purpose is to carry out the will of Satan...but, my purpose is to, with God's help and guidance, rebuke evil forces, and to win every battle that I come up against.

Now, I can't say that I was successful in doing this when I was younger. I didn't have the relationship that I now have with God. But, what I can say is that God was always there.

When I was almost raped by the bully boy at the age of seven, it was God that made little Bodie Ali fight her way out. And, honestly, I think it was, again, God who appeared before that boy, speaking to and/or frightening him into never trying to assault me again. Like I mentioned before, he had that look and continued to talk the talk...but, not once did he attempt to walk the walk.

As for my mother's friends and others who let their perverse spirits take charge, I'm glad that God saw to deliver me from those individuals. I would have never made it, had it not been for His grace. I would never have made it, had it not been for His mercy. And, because I know that there are many who don't make it, I am even that much more thankful for His love and hands upon my life.

You never know what goes through the minds of persons you feel closest to...but, NEVER put perversion past anyone. Women, men, boys and girls...all are subject to wrongful behaviors, simply because that's Satan's job – to kill, steal and destroy.

To the guys (and/or women) who get your rocks off fondling young children, or forcing someone against their will to perform sexual acts with you, I pray for your deliverance. I've already said that God doesn't like ugly. I've already said that God repays those who wrongfully and/or unjustly harm His children (especially those who call out to Him). I've already given you examples of what happened to those who wronged me. But, don't take my word for it. Keep on. And, when your days start counting down, I want you to remember these very words, as written in Isaiah 3:11 - *Woe to the wicked! Disaster is upon them! They will be paid back for what their hands have done.*

To the young girls and/or guys who may still be going through situations such as the ones I have, hold on.

You may be sick at your stomach. You may be disgusted beyond words. You may be tired and weary. But, hold on. You may feel like you've had it. You may feel like there's no hope. You may even feel like you're at the end of your rope. But, hold on.

There may be times when you truly believe there's no one to tell...there's nowhere to go...there's no one to offer comfort and/or encouragement... but, in those times, do as I did. Cry out to God, whether you know Him or not. Cry out to Him. He will hear you, and He will rescue you. As the scripture says, He will never leave you nor forsake you. That's His promise. Trust in that. Believe in that. Know that.

You will survive.

ROUND THREE:
DISTRACKTED

Always enjoyed weekend trips
and the time spent at my auntie's house.
The A-T-L was the place to be...
that's where I found my first real crush.
Tall, slender and very handsome...
he was like heaven to my eyes.
"I wasn't a virgin...I've had plenty" –
but, they were all lies.
Never got serious, never knew why,
never sought answers to that riddle.
Must have been something;
got children with his first name and middle.
Thirteen was about the age
in which I experienced puppy love.
He was seven years older than me,
but I still gave my innocence up.
Was having issues at home with mom,
so to my grandma's house I moved.
Little did she know, my puppy love was
right there with me, too.
Thought I was slick with my plans;
got away on several occasions.
But, one time I got caught...
why were they there? Who was that lady?
A lot of cursing, a lot of talking,

even rode out to the man's house.
At 2 am, he was threatened
and warned to stay away from Petty Drive.
The story didn't end there, though...
for I was quiet and somewhat sneaky.
Often called him, 'Spiderman',
cause two stories, he'd climb to see me.
Two whole years with no protection,
was thinking I didn't have to worry.
I was so much believing that,
that I was seeing him fairly often.
Even thought I'd play a hand
at adding another for the ride...
So, I had one in Marietta,
and another on the south side.
Thought I was doing it,
until my friend failed to pay her monthly visit.
Four whole months I tried to hide it,
until my pants no longer zipped.
Got yelled at for a while...
24 hours to be exact.
Abortion was the word spoken,
but hearing the heartbeat stopped all that.
"It's mine, and I'm keeping it"...
those were the words felt from my heart.
I loved that little seed...
was overjoyed at his birth.

Had an issue with paternity,
cause like I said, there were two.
The test proved negative on one,
but the other didn't believe the news.
Said my son's skin was too light,
and didn't look like him in any way.
That, along with an overnight stay,
made me dismiss all future claims.
Didn't feed my child much,
brought him soiled clothes instead of new.
My son was definitely worth more than that...
I will do what I have to do.
So "keep it moving" was the word...
"hope your child forgives you later."
Cause if he can't be your priority,
then you ain't worthy to be his daddy.
Used to think after having a child,
they would trust my better judgment.
But, yet, I never knew what it was
like to have a curfew past eleven.
Never got to go to my prom...
only been on about two or three dates...
Didn't even attend a high school football game
until after I had graduated.
It wasn't easy being a single mother,
especially one trying to finish school.
But, I was thankful for the opportunities
presented for me to be able to.

Everything went into place...
completed my education, and got a job.
Doors were often opened...
and I walked through them, one by one.
A hard mother, yes I was,
because that was the training that I received.
Afraid of me by the age of two,
but he was going to respect me.
Often watched folks raise their kids;
many shunned me for my style.
They just couldn't understand the
reasons why I never spared the rod.
But, that's ok, they see it now,
whether they want to admit it or not.
I had a young son who was respectful,
and never once cursed me out.
Never felt I was the best,
but a good mom I strived to be.
I had to do it for my son...
for he was a blessing sent to me.

**For every creature of God is good,
and nothing to be refused,
if it be received with thanksgiving**
1 Timothy 4:4 (KJV)

Fifteen.

And pregnant.

How did that happen, you say?

Life. And, my desperate attempt to find love.

No longer playing with dolls. Those were for kids. I'm a grown woman now. Don't you see my figure? This cute face, these perky breasts, tight little buns and shapely legs? You can't tell me you don't like me...or that you don't want me. I know you want to see what I'm about. What I'm holding. Whether it's tight or loose. Whether I can kiss or not. Whether I'm experienced or not.

I see you looking at me as I walk by. I know you like the way my skirt fits. I see you licking your lips. I'll even let you see me licking mine back. But, then what?

You call me over? You compliment me? I give you my number? You call me? We stay on the phone talking 'til the wee hours of the morning? We meet up at the mall? We go to the movies? You start letting your hands roam all over me? We sneak off? I let you have a taste? Without protection? We laugh about it?

But, uh oh...my cycle's late. I think I'm pregnant. Now what?

For many girls, this was the scenario. A cute young boy comes your way. It may be that classroom crush. It may be that jock on the football team. It may be the boy next door. Or, even the boy at church. But, regardless of where he's found, the point is, he's found.

He's handsome. Charming. Knows exactly what to say. Knows exactly how to act. Pretends to be just what we think we want. And, then, whalah! He has not only set the trap; but, he's managed to capture us, too.

But, wait. Some of us tend to get greedy. Why have just one? If he likes us, surely this other one will, too. We can tell they both want us. They both say they love us. So, why not?

Okay...that's my story. Two guys...after the same thing. They both appear sincere...they both say they love me...they both get to do me. Now, I have been called a lot of things...so, go ahead, take your stab, too, if you're feeling it. I knew it was wrong. But, at 14, when all you can think of are these cute, young boys whispering in your ear, and what they mean and/or bring into your life, I had to do it. They loved me, and I loved them. Or, so I thought.

After two years of having unprotected sex, and a few months of playing the field and having sexual relations with two guys, I think I'm pregnant.

My cycle didn't come this month. So, I faked it. Ketchup on sanitary napkins, so my grandmom wouldn't get suspicious.

My cycle didn't come the next month, either. Uh oh. It's on now! I thought I got a beat down for two hickeys being on my neck...wonder what I'll get for being pregnant.

I'm nervous. I tell one of the guys that I think I'm pregnant. He laughs. I tell the other guy and he curses me out and calls me stupid. Me...stupid? Oh, I guess I did it to myself. I guess he had nothing at all to do with me getting pregnant. O. K.

Well, four months have gone by, and now I can no longer zip my pants. If I could just come up with $175, I could get an abortion and my mom would never know. But, something kept telling me to just go ahead and tell her. Just tell her...you're pregnant. Go on and get it over with. Do it now. So, I did.

"Mama, I gotta talk to you about something...in private."

So, we go to my room, shut the door, and I proceed to tell her that although I know how she's going to react, I needed for her to understand that I didn't mean for it to happen. So, I told her. I told her I thought I was pregnant, because my period hadn't come in four months. She sat there and looked at me for a minute. Then, asked who the daddy was. At the time, I told her it was the guy she knew who lived near us. She immediately starting making me feel about two feet tall. She commenced to yelling (not hitting, this time...thank goodness), but yelling. She called me every name except for the one listed on my birth certificate. She even talked trash about the guy. And, then said she was going to take me to the doctor the next day to see about getting an abortion, because she didn't want me ruining my life, or having to quit school.

The next day came. We went to the E.R. They took a urine sample. My pregnancy test came back positive. They laid me on a table, rubbed this jelly substance on my stomach, and ran this cold metal object all around my abdomen. I heard the strangest sounds – whoosh, whoosh, thump thump, thump thump, whoosh, whoosh, thump thump. The nurse said that was the baby's heartbeat. I smiled.

The nurse told my mom that if I was going to get an abortion, I only had about a week or so left to do it. I told my mom – then – I wasn't having an abortion; but, that instead, I was going to keep it. So, that was the plan. And, I stuck with it.

Family members were notified. A lot of them were shocked, but all understood. After all, just about all of the women in my family, including my mom and grandmom, had had children in their teens and/or out of wedlock...so, what would make me so different?

I still stayed in school, however, as dropping out was not an option, nor a desire. Yeah, it felt funny walking around school with a big belly; but, it wasn't as bad, once I noticed a few other girls doing the same thing. At an eight-month doctor's visit, I was told I had developed toxemia – pregnancy-induced high blood pressure, which was causing my ankles and hands to swell. They said they would have to induce my labor early, if I hadn't delivered within a week. I went into labor two days before that scheduled procedure.

A quick labor...but, the pain was immense. Nothing that I could have ever imagined. Nothing that I ever wanted to feel again. I delivered naturally – no drugs, no anesthesia. But, that end result...after that last push...out came what I had always prayed for...a sweet, little, healthy baby boy.

Tears falling from my eyes, at the sight of him. Joy in my heart, at the touch of him. God is good! I was good...

...until it came time to call his father (or both of them, since I didn't yet know whose child he actually was).

I called the first guy...and after arriving at the hospital, and visiting my son in the nursery, he immediately claimed that my son wasn't his child. Something about my son's skin color being almost white and he being jet black (like me being light- skinned couldn't play a part in my son being light-skinned).

The other guy came to visit a couple of days later and immediately became ecstatic, saying my son looked just like him. If only you could have seen the joy that was all over *his* face. He went into daddy mode really quick...talking all of that "I'm going to take him here, take him there" talk. That was really nice to hear. And, I was up for that.

But, my conscious wouldn't let me let him continue with those thoughts, until I knew for sure that he was the father. It was only right.

Besides, I had to be sure. So, I asked him to participate in a blood test. He did. The test came back 99.99% *negative*. He was not the father. I almost died. I just knew (or more like I was really hoping) that he was my son's father. He had to be. He took to my son like he knew all along. His family took to my son. They even gave him his first nickname. How could I hurt them that way? How could I hurt my son that way?

Now, the people who have grown attached to him, and who he had grown attached to, would no longer be around. I found it funny how quickly they detached themselves after hearing the news; but, I understood...totally.

Shortly after getting the results, I went to inform the other guy of the test, telling him that he was indeed the father...all he had to say was, "Yeah, ok...I'll do what I can do when I can do it."

Well...I never saw any diapers being delivered. Or any clothes being bought. Or any milk being supplied. Or any money being exchanged from his hands to mine. All I recognized was his attempts to keep 'kicking it' with me, without even a thought about our son. So, I asked myself, and then I asked him, just when it was he was 'planning' to do what it was he could do?

Two years later, he finally wanted to keep our son for a weekend. So, I let him, while at the same time informing him that our son needed some clothes. I went to pick my son up on Sunday, only to find him dirty and not looking right. I asked my son what he ate, and all he said was, 'rice.' I took the bag of used clothing that his father gave me, and while smiling at the thought of his father actually trying to do something for our son, I immediately got sick at the smell coming from a pair of soiled shorts that were in the bag. What did he do? Take some young boy's clothes right off of his body?

I grew ill. Ill at the fact that my son wasn't good enough to have clean clothes being given to him. Ill at the fact that my son was not taken care of and/or fed properly. Ill at the fact that this man insisted on being in my life, still getting the good-good, but was nowhere near interested in taking care of his seed.

So ill that I was forced to make a choice for him. I told him that since my son's well-being was of no interest to him, that he could walk...and forget that he even had a son by me. I would be the mama, and play the daddy...I would do all *I* could to take care of my son. Yeah, I knew my son needed a father in his life; but, he wasn't going to get it in a man who would rather hang out on the streets selling dope, hollering at every piece of fresh meat that walked by, and who was constantly going in and out of jail. So, as I mentioned, I did what *I* had to do.

Thanks to my mother being a stay-at-home mom, I was able to graduate from both high school and a technical school, while she watched my son for me. I landed my first real job as a secretary at a local hospital, and continued to move up from there.

I was determined, with opportunities being presented by God, to make it. I had to make it...for my son's sake. I had to keep going...to feed us...to clothe us...to keep a shelter over our heads. I had to continue on...even when times got rough, cause that little boy was depending on me.

Now, I wasn't an easy mom; as a matter of fact, in my early motherhood years, I found myself being just like my mom was towards me. My son literally caught hell growing up. Child abused...yeah, he was. But, he lived. Yelled and cursed at...yeah, he was. But, he got over it. Over and over again. Until, one day, God spoke to me...saying, 'Bodie, love him.' So, I changed up a bit. I tried to do the things that would make him respect me, not fear me...talk to me, not disregard me...love me, not hate me.

There were many strategies in which I could have taken. There are still things – to this day – that I am learning to do or not to do; but, I'm thankful that God has helped me, along the way, to nurture and support him...and to help him grow into the fine young man he is today.

Now, I'm not saying that all scenarios turn out this way...some girls are nowhere near mother material at such a young age...but, I'm grateful for the wisdom that God gave me, as it truly helped in my quest to *raise* my child, not just have him.

While many have given me a hard time about being a single teen mother, there were some who gave me kudos for being the type of mother that I was. They said that I was much more mature than other mothers my age. That I had a good head on my shoulders. That I was going to go places and do things. That my son would be proud of me.

Well, all I can say is that I tried...my best. I made sure he never wanted for anything. I made sure he was taken care of. I made sure he had food and/or a little money when spending the night over to relatives and friends' houses. I tried my best to make it so he wouldn't have to depend on anyone or anything out there in the streets. I encouraged good behavior and decent grades. I demanded respect to me and all of his elders. I promoted his manhood, and always tried to give sound advice. And, most importantly, I did my best to show him that he was *loved*.

Even today.

And, I am blessed to be able to say that through all of his years of living at home, he has never been a bother, or a burden or a nuisance. He was pleasant and always obedient. You know they always say, 'what goes around comes around.' And, I am sure that my being respectful and obedient to my mom played a major part in me getting the same treatment from *my* son. Thank God for His favor!

My Pride and Joy

A heart beat was all it took...
to make me fall in love with you.
The thought of seeing your face...
gave me strength to carry you.

To hear you call me 'mama'
brought straight tears to my eyes.
Seeing you take your first steps
literally made me cry.

A smart young boy with a handsome smile –
able to melt the hardest of hearts.
Shy and to yourself,
but your respectfulness was always tops.

From Pre-K to College,
you've proven yourself to be...
a fine young man
who can be whatever he so dreams.

From the day that you were born
until my day to leave this earth,
I stand proudly to claim to all
that you are my pride and joy...

Do all that you can do...
Be all that you can be.
Keep first the love of God,
and remember the love of me.

Recoil...

Remember when I said that all things happen for a reason? Well, there was definitely a reason for my becoming a mother at the age of 15. My son was a blessing...sent from God Himself. He was given life so that I could become the woman I am today, instead of the woman I almost was [had it not been for the seed that was placed inside of me].

In everything that we go through, and in everything that comes before us, there is always a purpose behind it. A plan that only God knows of, that only God understands...until, of course, He has chosen to reveal to us just why it was we were chosen to go through whatever it was we were going through.

Teen-aged pregnancies these days are about as common as teens smoking cigarettes in the past. The only difference is that one becomes a habit, and the other is a gift, or at least is supposed to be a gift.

I say 'supposed to' because there are some who think getting pregnant while still in their teens is the worst thing that could possibly happen...a mistake that can only be corrected by having an abortion. Or, for some, having children is just another means to get the government to pay for their hair and nails to be done, or that new pair of shoes they've been wanting. And, then, there are some who, if they even chose to have the child, are not dedicated enough to take care of them in the way God would have them; they won't provide that child with the love, support and protection that he or she so richly deserves and so desperately needs.

And, then, there are those like me...who are thankful for the blessing to just be able to have a child. Thankful that God chose me to procreate, and trusted me to raise a child who can be used for good on this earth.

Now, I can't sit here and tell you that I wasn't scared. I was...very much so. But, without God giving me the love, courage and confidence that I needed, I'm sure I would not have been able to completely fulfill most missions that were set before me. Losing in this thing called motherhood was not an option for me; and, I knew I had to rely, trust in and embrace God's loving hands, if I was to win. Thank God for his grace!

He said to be fruitful and to multiply...that I did. He said to trust in Him, knowing that whatever He has planned, it was planned for my good. I knew that. And, I believed that.

My son was indeed my pride and joy, and I loved him with everything I had. And, although I wasn't a perfect mother, I always tried my best to be a good one. He never had to want for anything. He was always able to get the things he wanted and/or asked for. We had a relationship unlike many, because even while I remained mama when he acted up, I was also big sister when it came to talking to and showing him the ways of life.

His friends and some family members were envious. Some actually said he was spoiled. But, I didn't see it that way. I saw him as a good kid who didn't manage to press my buttons as frequently as most kids pressed their parents. I saw a lot of myself in him. The same values I had while growing up, I could see in him. As a matter of fact, he was so much like me that it was almost scary.

He had a sensitive side, a caring side, an understanding side, an obedient side...all of the characteristics that a mother could want...which truly made being a teen-age mother easy. And, for that, I was thankful.

I am still thankful.

To those folks who tend to look down on teen mothers just because they're *teen* mothers, shame on you. Of course, the timing couldn't be worse. Of course, they may have no idea of how to go about raising a child. Of course, they might not even be in a position to take care of a child. But, there was a reason that God allowed for that seed to be planted. There was a reason that God protected that seed from its conception to its birth. And, there was a reason that God made that young mother and/or father parents when He did.

Children are not mistakes. Never mistakes. And, anyone who thinks so is completely blind to the miracles of God. Or, perhaps, just blind to God, period. As noted in Psalm 127:3-4, "Children are a gift from the Lord; babies are a reward. Children who are born to a young man are like arrows in the hand of a warrior."

Now, don't get it twisted. I didn't throw that scripture there to prove that it's ok for youngsters to have children. I don't think that's what it was saying. My point was to confirm my statement that children are gifts from God.

And, by no means do I condone teen-age pregnancy; nor, do I like to see young folks get themselves into that predicament. I would much rather they waited until they were married to have children...or, married before having sex, period. But, the reality, nowadays, is that that is so far from the norm, that it would only be hopeful wishing on my part.

But, what I am is understanding to the fact that a child being brought into this world by a young teen mother and father is not a mistake. I say this because, I, once, was a teen-aged mother, and I understand. I understand that things happen. And, now that I've grown into adulthood, and have had another son (through marriage), I can see the bigger picture.

God uses us to multiply...and age, to Him, is of no value, when He has a plan. No one knows the purpose for Him allowing that young girl to become impregnated. No one knows just how that child is going to change that mother and/or father's life. No one knows just how God will use that mother, father or child to carry out His mission. So, why should we jump to conclusions and automatically speak failure into their lives?

My advice to everyone in any situation would be to stop trying to play God. Stop trying to crucify young girls, just because they couldn't keep their legs closed. Stop trying to hang those young men, just because they don't – yet – know how to be a father. Stop speaking death unto that child's life.

God is the only one who can place judgment. Your job is to love – regardless and in spite of. Instead of making the teens feel lower than the dirt they walk on, uplift them. Teach them. Nurture and protect them; so, that they will, in turn, know how to love, nurture and protect the child that God has blessed them with. God called us to be examples...or, better yet, witnesses. He didn't call us to be condemners. And, I believe once we get that little-known fact deeply engraved into our brain cells (and heart), we will become a better people.

So, again, love them.

As for you young women...who find yourselves to be so tempting...so pretty...so smart...and able to turn most, if not all heads, you better make sure his stuff is wrapped up. I won't dare sit and tell you that you better not have sex...or that you better stop talking to and/or flirting with those cute-but-no-good-for-you boys. But, what I will tell you is that life is too short and too precious to let slip right through your hands. If you become pregnant, it could only mean one of three things:

1) You voluntarily laid down with some guy – unprotected.
2) You failed to take and/or use your contraceptives correctly. Or,
3) You were forced against your will to spread'em.

Now, aside from the third scenario, the other two are totally preventable. First off, you should never have unprotected sex with anyone. Never mind about getting pregnant. That could be the least of your worries. How about contracting HIV, Herpes, Chlamydia, Syphilis, or any of the other body- and life-threatening sexually transmitted diseases?

Though some can be handled through a shot or a series of pills, there *are* those that can result in your sterility, or even your death. And, the sad part about it all is that you probably don't even know how to have sex well enough to enjoy it. It's just something that everyone else is doing, so you feel you gotta fit in. Or, it's something that your boyfriend told you to do to prove that you loved him.

Love. Now, that's a strong word. If you loved him? What about if he loved you? If he loved you, he wouldn't keep trying to get you to do something that you're not comfortable with and/or ready for. If he loved you, he would protect himself *and* you by insisting that he wraps it up. Condoms are really cheap these days...especially when you consider the alternatives of not using them – like having to raise a child or living with a life-threatening disease.

Now, I know what I'm saying might be 'going in one ear and out the other,' as the old folk used to say...but, take it from someone who's been there and done that.

I'm guilty. Guilty of having unprotected sex – repeatedly. Guilty of contracting one sexually transmitted disease after another. Guilty of getting pregnant at the age of 15, and out of wedlock. Just guilty. But, what I finally realized is that through it all, what I was most guilty of was not loving myself enough to take care of myself.

No young boy or man is worth losing your sanity or life over. Even if they're the finest boy in the school. Even if you've been dating him for months, and he says all the right things...does all the right things...seems like the 'one'. And, I know you've heard of celibacy until marriage; but, I also know you've probably somehow managed to convince yourself that you can't hold out that long, or that that Prince Charming will leave you for someone else, if you don't give it up. Right! Some Prince Charming. Sounds more like Mr. Hyde, if you ask me.

But, anyway.

If you get nothing else out of this chapter, please get this: You are a child of God. And, whatever you choose to do – remain celibate, have protected sex, or continue having unprotected sex – know that they are *your* choices. You can either choose to sleep peacefully in a nice, pillow-top, king sized wonder bed, or choose to sleep on a hard, wooden cot. In other words, you can make your bed hard, or you can make it soft...the choice is – always – up to you.

But, realize that not all outcomes from your choices will be to your benefit. Not all will bring joy into your life. Not all will affect just you. So, choose...but, choose carefully.

I am giving this same advice to my young men out there. If you've made it this far, you've read all of what I had to say to the young women. It is all relevant to you and your well-being, as well.

Some of you may feel like you're Rico Suavey...like no one can touch your swag...like you're the Trey Songz or Chris Brown of your city or town, or state (if your head is that big)...but, trust me when I say, you are 'nothing' if you lay with a girl – unprotected, get her pregnant, and then, not own up to your half of the doing. You will be seen as less than a man...by that girl *and* that child (when he or she grows up). You will be judged by your Heavenly father, who is always watching you...always taking a count of each and every last one of your actions.

And, just in case you didn't know, God made men to be leads...to be providers...to be protectors. If you can't do these things, you are not the man God called you out to be. If God has blessed you with the ability to give life, and you don't take care of that life, trust me when I say, your day of chastisement is coming.

You may not get it from your parents. You may not get it from the girl you got pregnant. You may not even get it from the child that you made. But, you will get it. God will see to that.

How do I know? Because I've seen it happen. Because I've heard stories. Because it says it in His Word. Everything done in the dark will come to light. All will give an account for his doings while here on earth. All will come up against the wrath of God...but, depending on their walk, some will be lucky enough to not have to experience that wrath.

The best thing for you to do is abstain. But, I know...that hormone just won't let you. So, ok then, the next best thing is to wrap it up. I know you can do that, *right*?!

Yeah, I know you might want to feel the real thing. Yeah, I know that it ain't love making if you and the girl aren't able to enjoy each other without restrictions. But, I also know that your ability to continue having sex long after the next time will depend on your ability to protect yourself this time. You, too, have to value yourself, your life, and your contribution to your generation. You, as a man, have some rather big shoes to fill; but, you can do it.

And, if you so happen to find out that you weren't as strong as you thought you were, at least...at very least, be man enough to take care of your responsibility. After all, if you were 'man' enough to lie down and get her pregnant, you should be man enough to obtain work to help take care of her and your baby. At very least.

And, if you're looking at a girl thinking she ain't future material, please spare yourself the possible headaches...and leave her alone. Don't have sex with her just to have sex with her...just to add another number to your stats. Sex is meant to be between 'lovers.' And, if you don't love her, you shouldn't be *doing* her. Ya feel me? And, if you don't love her enough to remain by her side, regardless and in spite of (meaning, if she gets pregnant or not), then, you shouldn't be having unprotected sex with her.

And, that's only right. If you start off handling your business in the right way, you won't have to worry about dealing with the consequences of the wrong way later...because, trust me, there will be consequences. And, not all consequences end up being good ones. It all depends on the choice you make.

That goes for the young women, as well.

In life, there will always be opportunities for you to mess up; but, that doesn't mean that God can't help you fix it. You may also be stubborn and hard headed one too many times; but, that doesn't mean that God won't give you another chance. You may even be proven young and naive; but, that has no bearing on God's ability to show you his favor by giving you the strength, courage and knowledge needed to handle your business.

I can say these things, because God has shown me these things.

You can succeed; but, you've got to start now. You can overcome; but, you've got to know how. You can do the right thing; but, you've got to want to.

It's not hard. For you young parents who don't know and/or are unsure of how to go about doing what you need to do, ask. There are so many of us elders who would love nothing more than to help you...to guide you in the right direction...to give you sound advice about parenting, and becoming a respected adult.

As a young parent, you're going to need all of the help you can get discerning between what's best to do versus what just sounds or seems right...or, how to go about showing your child unconditional love versus being selfish and ugly towards them. Never forget that YOU were the one who made it possible for them to be here. If you didn't want to deal with the sometimes hard and burdensome task of raising a child, you should have made a better choice! That's a consequence.

And, if you just got mad at me for making that statement, it's young folk like you that I pity. Those of you who think you know it all already – my only advice to you at this moment in your life is to pray, cause you're going to need it when you fall flat on your face. And, I didn't say that to be mean...I said that because it's true. One day, in some way, your selfish and immature ways of thinking are going to catch up with you...forcing you to put your foot in your mouth...and leaving you with the thoughts, 'if only I had just listened.'

All it takes is a moment...to mess up. You will experience quite a few ups and downs when raising a child. You may even find yourself struggling often to make ends meet, or working tirelessly to try to meet the demands of raising that child. As I've warned before, you can either make your bed hard, or you can make it soft. You can listen to advice, or you can learn the hard way. You can have child after child, or you can learn from the first one. You can be a great parent, or one that your child will grow to resent. All of which are – again - your choices.

Question is...will you make the right one?

ROUND FOUR:
VOWS UNDUN

We all dream of it...all think about it...
all wonder just how it would be...
To find that person with whom
you could live the rest of your life with.
Characteristics should be complementary,
able to make your soul sing.
So, just why did I get caught up,
only to end up settling?
Heard the warnings...saw the signs...
but, I was so tired of instability.
They kept saying he wouldn't change;
but I was confident in my abilities.
Didn't like him from the start,
or what he stood for when we met.
Gold tooth, an arrogant nature...
my spirit ached and quickly fled.
Four years later – our next encounter...
he seemed better than before.
Didn't have anybody serious...
so, I decided to take a chance.
There was drama, constant arguing,
a trust level well below the norm.
Yet, I still thought his commitment
would keep my heart from getting hurt.

A thoughtless way to propose,
but I accepted and started planning.
Funding the entire wedding with monies
he wouldn't even give me.
Times were often very trying...
found myself wanting to call it off.
But, the embarrassment was enough
to make him beg for me not.
Fully dressed...but, I kept hearing
my spirit constantly screaming, 'NO.'
It took all I had to ignore it...
cause getting married was my goal.
No first dance, no song to remember...
I was even left at the church.
Asked my pastor for an annulment,
cause right then, I felt the hurt.
Honeymoon was good though,
seeing how we were both under the influence.
But, as soon as we got back home,
the drama yet continued.
In addition to the lack of trust,
insecurities began creeping my way.
How could he resist his sexy wife
to watch a movie he could replay?
Emotional affairs I often had
cause my needs were not being met.
Yeah, he might have won the trophy...
but, it was obviously valueless.

Never dusted it, never admired it,
never even blinked another eye.
Truly clueless about his duties
and obligations to his wife.
Would have monthly conversations
to reveal my unhappiness.
Kool-aid stains painted the walls,
as all my feelings were dismissed.
Self-esteem at an all-time low,
didn't know what else I could possibly do.
Was just about to leave this man,
until came along, seed number two.
A sweet little baby boy...
everything was going good at first.
Until he let his friend enter our home
without me first getting dressed.
What on earth was he thinking?
Why would he expose his wife like that?
Temptation is truly dangerous
when emotions are not in check.
Roaming eyes and frequent thoughts
led me to asking for separation.
Cause it was only a matter of time
until someone finally convinced me.
Let him back in a few months later,
cause he said he'd found God.
Only to find that his 'religion'
would tear us further and further apart.

He might have changed in some of his ways,
but it wasn't what I needed.
My spirit was seriously hurting...
deeply wounded and constantly bleeding.
On my knees one lonesome night...
I managed to cry my last cry.
Asked God for His mercy,
cause I was leaving for real this time.
Informed my ex-husband of my decision
and was labeled a non-Christian.
Cause "divorce was not an option;
God would never, ever forgive me."
A chance I swore to take.
One month later, he was served.
Officially divorced in five months...
last name changed back to the first.
Wasn't happy getting married,
but was thrilled with getting divorced.
Praying that God would eventually guide me
into finding my true love.

**To everything there is a season,
and a time to every purpose under the heaven:**

Ecclesiastes 3:1 (KJV)

Marriage.

It could be the best thing that ever happened to you, or it can be the worst. It can prove to be a wonderful fairytale, or a horrible nightmare. It can be fruitful and full of growth, or it can be stunted and short lived.

It can be...whatever you make it.

Question is...what will you make it? What will your spouse make it? Will the two of you agree? Or, will you fall apart? Will you sacrifice and compromise? Or, will you be stubborn and set in your ways? Will you be the man or woman God made you to be? Or, will you think that His ways are unobtainable? Will you love your spouse 'til death do you part? Or, will you leave when times get rough?

All of these were questions that ran through my mind...before I got married, while I was married, and after I got divorced.

Divorce.

It could be the best thing that ever happened to you, or it can be the worst. It could end peacefully, or it could end tragically. It can be mutual, or it can be contested. There could be disturbances in the kids, or they could be just fine. You could be financially set for life, or in someone's bankruptcy court. Your in-laws could hate you, or they could still love you.

Whatever the case...there are pros and cons to both – being married or getting divorced. The question is...which one will it be for you?

For me, marriage was not what I had expected. There were several key ingredients that my marriage was lacking; so, divorce was the better choice – for me. But, my story, like so many others, was based upon lies that I had told myself...in the beginning.

'He will change. We will get better. I'm in love with him. I can see myself
with him for the rest of my life. He won't cheat on me once we're
married. I can be all that he needs me to be. He completes me. I can
tame his temper. We are compatible. He loves my child. He loves me.
His family will accept me. I can deal with his baby mama. I can accept his
child. We will have ups and downs, but, nothing will come between us.
Our beliefs and values will remain the same, and we will agree on more
than we disagree on. We both believe in God and He will keep us
together; why else would He allow us to marry each other? We are
meant for each other.'

Every one of those statements, I have said or at some point thought.
And, although I wasn't quite sure if we would truly be together for the
rest of our lives, I was determined to give it a shot. You see, I wanted to
be married. I wanted to walk down the aisle in my little white dress. I
wanted to live that fairytale life. After all, we had already been living
together for almost two years...so, really, we were already pretty much
married. Right?

Wrong. Or, at least not according to my spirit. From day one (of me
meeting my ex-husband), my spirit was always screaming, 'No! Don't do
it! Stop! Think! Let it go!'

And you know, the spirit is a funny thing. Some people call it intuition.
Some call it a gut feeling. Some call it a voice in their head. I call it, God.

We always ask for and want to hear Him talk to us...guide us...confirm to
us whether or not we're making the right choice, going in the right
direction, doing the right thing. We're always asking for signs and
wonders....and, then when He answers and/or shows us [sometimes,
time after time], we don't want to see, hear and/or listen to Him. We
want to ignore the voice. We want to think it's the devil talking. We
want to seek fortune tellers and palm readers to tell us what to do.
When all the time, God is speaking to us...clearly.

My previous marriage was nowhere near rose petals and candlelight; but, looking back over everything, I realized that it did serve a purpose...which was to teach me...to listen.

I can sit here and try to paint a perfect picture for you. But, it's not in my best interest [or yours] to lie. I could sit here and tell you that I was to blame for all of the bad things that happened in my previous marriage. But, I wouldn't dare jeopardize my reputation by speaking falsely in my own book. I could sit here and tell you that I only thought about getting divorced once during that marriage. But, why lie? Truth is – divorce was on the brain and the tongue as soon as I realized he left me at the church.

Yes. You read it correctly. He left me at the church. Apparently, someone forgot that we were going to leave from the church together in his car to head to our honeymoon destination. So, I was left driving home in a small, two-door export dressed in a bulky, traditional style wedding dress. Very nice, I tell ya. Very nice.

Now, I won't sit here and tell you that all of the time spent with my ex-husband was bad. Out of a combined 44,165 days together, there were roughly 6,670 good ones.

For the longest, I used to think that perhaps it was my perception. Perhaps I just expected too much. Perhaps I wanted too much. Perhaps I wasn't good enough for him. Perhaps he was more man than I could handle. Perhaps...

...he just wasn't the 'ONE.'

It's every woman's wish to have that prince charming or knight in shining armor come rescue her from the trials of the world, and then whisk her away into the sunset to live happily ever after. Heck, who wouldn't want that? But, the reality is...there is no prince charming or knight in shining armor...there are only men. Sometimes good men. Sometimes bad men.

Mine...was a man...raised in a small little country town. Two parent household. Baby boy of about 10 kids. Grew up in a Holiness church. One baby mama. One child. A steady job. His own place. His own car. Attractive. Experienced in bed. Quick Tempered. Frugal.

Me...a woman...raised all over metro-Atlanta. One parent household. Oldest of four kids. Grew up in a Methodist church. One baby daddy. One child. A steady job. My own place. My own car. Attractive. Experienced in bed. Laid Back. Generous.

Now, to hear the stats, one would think that we had enough commonalities and enough differences to have a lasting and fruitful bond. But, something somewhere went completely wrong.

I thought I was a good wife. Went to work, came home, cooked dinner, washed clothes, spoke nicely, showed tons of affection, gave him space, watched the games, planned intimate trips, prayed, had his child, paid the bills, helped him obtain two houses, supported his efforts, sexed him when he wanted, no addictions or bad habits, carried myself well. So, what else was I missing?

Why the lack of affection? Why the lack of attention? Why the lack of initiative?

Was there someone else? Did I not appeal to his senses? Was I a bother to him? Was he in the closet? Did he no longer want to be married? What? What?

For years, I asked myself these same questions. For years, I would sit down and have conversations with him to try to figure out what was going on...what was going wrong...to let him know how I was feeling...to see if and/or how we could make things better. For years...I tried.

I had tried for so long that I began losing touch with myself, with what I wanted, with what I needed. Bodie didn't do anything if he didn't want to do it. Bodie didn't go anywhere if he didn't want to go. Bodie didn't bother him if he didn't want to be bothered. Self-esteem – at an all-time low. Desire to be married – completely gone. Spirit – wounded. Will to continue on – shot.

I used to wonder if he not getting to continue his relationship with a childhood female friend was the reason. I never said he couldn't talk to her...just told him that either she was going to acknowledge and respect me, or one of us had to go. Either she was going to call our home [and not his cell] to talk to him, or she wasn't going to call at all. I mean, I didn't see what the problem was, seeing how they'd been friends since they could both remember.

Childhood friends who can't call your house [now that you're married] – to me – spelled something more to it. He would swear nothing had ever happened...but, I'm a woman. And, I know women. So, either they had something deeper in the past and she still had feelings, or she had feelings that she never let surface. Whatever the case, I refused to be treated as if my feelings didn't matter...as if I was second to her. I told him he could have her. I told him he could leave. But, he insisted he loved me and only me. Right!

Guess that's the reason why I caught him in another woman's house...instead of waiting outside for me to get home. My neighbor. Wow. They always say you should watch your enemies, but I think you should watch your so-called friends closer.

Now, let him tell it, he was just there watching the game (until I got home to unlock the door). And, she was just cleaning her house in a t-shirt. And, because she had her kids running around, "there was no way anything could have happened." All of this being said while he had a sister living not even 10 yards away (who was at home, mind you); but, perhaps, she wouldn't have let him watch the game in her house. Yeah, that's it!

Well, luckily for her (and him), God didn't let certain things play out in a certain order. Because, had I had known – at the time – that she was a snake who liked preying on her friends' husbands, I believe she would have truly felt my wrath...and he would have completely felt my pain.

More and more acts had me growing weary by the day. There's only so far you can go...so much you can take...so long you can deal with and/or handle being disrespected...disregarded... dishonored.

I used to do all I could do to put a smile on his face...to make things easy for and on him...to bring to his life contentment and satisfaction...

I would bring a sexiness that most men would find extremely difficult to ignore. I mean, how can one turn away his almost naked, naturally seductive, sexually aroused wife to watch a movie that he could rewind and play again later? I felt I was being thoughtful enough to not bother him during a play-off game, etc...but, I guess I failed to realize that movies were in the same ranking. Shame on me.
 Another one of my shamefuls was being too attentive. I listened – carefully. I watched – often. I bought – his wishes. I did – the unthinkable. I tried – always.

I paid close attention to what he said his desires were, what he wanted to have, where he wanted to go. But, when I would say, "sweetie, I don't like stuffed animals and chocolates," for years, I would continue to get stuffed animals and chocolates. When I say, "honey, I love red roses", not one did he buy for me. Even the clothes he tried to buy...he knew they weren't my style. But, it was always the thought that I was supposed to count, right?

Moving on....

For five years, I had been asking him if we could start trying for a child together...cause I always wanted two children (which he knew before even proposing to me). His reply was always 'not right now.' So, ok. I thought I'd fix things for him. He didn't love me. He didn't cherish me. He didn't edify me. He didn't fulfill me. He didn't want to give me a child. That spelled, he didn't want to be married to me anymore.
So, I had a long, long talk with God one day...informing Him that I was at my wits end... that I couldn't take it anymore...that my ex-husband wasn't being the husband I needed...that although I didn't want to make the wrong decision, I might just do so if He doesn't show me a sign of some sort...and soon.

Two weeks later, that sign came. I was pregnant.

"Guess you want me to stay, huh, Lord?" "Guess the joke is on me, huh, Lord?"

Alright. I'm here. I'm staying. After all, I've *got* to see what it is You're making me stay here for. I'm going to see if this negro is going to change...if he's going to get and do better...if he is going to be the man I need him to be.

A few months into my pregnancy, my ex-husband's father passes away. And, I, being a graphic designer (by hobby), was asked to handle the design and printing of his father's obituaries. So, during one of the family's funeral planning sessions, I went around the room asking for details to include in the obituary, along with the correct names of all of the children, etc. My ex-husband was not in the room.

While reiterating and confirming all of the information that was given to me, I stated my ex-husband's full name (since I already knew that), and the whole room got quiet. All of my ex-husband's sisters looked at me as if I had turned into Satan. One even yelled out, "where did you get that middle name from? He ain't got no middle name...you've been married to him this long and you don't know that?!!"

Five years being married to this man. Every document from our marriage certificate to our life insurance papers to the title on our house had this middle name stamped on it. A name that he told me was his middle name. A name I could never say out loud, due to it also being my first crush's middle name. Can you say, furious? To be sitting in a room full of his elder siblings who are looking at you like you don't even know your own spouse...like you've been married for five years, and you haven't seen or obtained proof of such things as important as his name. Can you say, blood boiling?

The reason I received – after angrily questioning him later, was that he always wanted that name, so he just gave himself that name. Another thing I found he lied about was the year he was born in. He had always said one year, but, his state driver's license said another. He claimed, then, that the DMV typed his birth year in wrong; but, during the three renewal periods that we were together, he always managed to forget to have his birth year corrected. Hmmm. My only question was, 'did I not deserve to know the truth?'

Well, I got over that fiasco...informing him that if I found one more important detail that he's lied about, I was going to immediately go and file for a divorce...on the grounds of false identity. And, I meant that [for those of you who may be thinking I was just playing].

A few more months passed, and my second child was finally born. Another sweet little baby boy. Yeah, I prayed for another boy, and was, as with my first child's birth, overjoyed at his birth. My ex-husband seemed happy, as well; and, didn't say a word when I gave our son that middle name he so desperately wanted and always liked. Now you're probably saying, 'ah, that was nice.' But, I didn't give that name to my son because my ex-husband liked the name; I did it out of spite. In my mind, I was giving him my first crush's middle name. I felt that would be payback to my ex-husband for lying all of those years; but, in reality, it was shame on me...because, now, I can't even say my son's middle name without having those thoughts.

But, anyway...that's a story for another time. Let me get back to the topic of the moment...

For the first few weeks after having my son, everything seemed to be going great. There was love in the house...affection in the house...understanding in the house...someone was really trying. I could almost say, I was happy...until that morning he let a friend come into our home, knowing I wasn't dressed for the occasion.

Let me paint the picture: I had on a pair of short shorts and a spaghetti-strapped, see-through camisole with no bra. And, because I was nursing at that time, my breasts were a little engorged with nipples erect. I was sitting on the sofa braiding my sister's hair...and he allows his friend to come in and sit right in front of me [while he remained out on the porch]. Somebody, please help me with this one!

Was he trying to push the dude on me? Was he trying to see if one of us would make a move on the other? What was the deal? Really! I asked, and his response was he 'hadn't noticed...he was sorry.' Wow!

Well, from that point...things started getting back to the norm...of what I was used to before I had our son. I knew it was too good to be true...and, was convinced that there was no changing an old dog. He's gonna be what he's always been. He's gonna do what he's always done.

Ok, Lord...now what?

A couple of years go by, and I take notice to the fact that I'm the only one buying groceries, buying our son's clothes, etc...and the sad part about it is that I, many times, had to use credit cards to do so (because my money was scarce). But, I overheard a conversation one day between he and his daughter's mother saying he could give her $100, after just giving her $80 a couple of weeks prior. What?!

"I thought you didn't have any money! If you got $100 to be giving away, why can't you put groceries on the table?"

His reply, "I gotta take care of my daughter!"

"Oh. Oh, I see. You gotta take care of your near grown daughter, but you ain't bought your son not even a pair of socks in the past three years." Oh. Ok.

His reply, "I pay the mortgage. I'm putting a roof over his head!"

Now, y'all...to know me would be to know that that statement alone was grounds enough to bust his ego...which I'm not even the type to do...but, on that day, I had to. I had to let him know that whether he was there or not, his son would have a roof over his head. And, that that was no excuse for not helping out with other things around the house, such as putting food on the table or occasionally chipping in to help with the needs of his son (ie, childcare, clothes, etc.).

I started feeling like I was a single parent again. Like I had had another son that I was going to be forced to take care of and raise alone...and the funny thing about this time is that I thought I had gotten it right. After all, I was still married and living with his father. Heck, if he didn't want the child, he should have just let me go when I was trying.

Lord, what is the lesson in this one? Perhaps, I misread the signs. Please tell me something.

To continue with the agony, there were always family functions (dinners and the like), or invitations to friends' houses, or other things going on/places I wanted to visit, that he didn't. I had to go alone (if it was my desire to go). He wasn't going. He never went. All he wanted to do was stay home...and watch television.

Well, my family caught on to that one real early. "Where's your husband this time?" "Why is he never with you?" "You all having problems?"

"What's really going on? You don't look happy." "Does he not know how many guys are out here trying to hit on you?"

Some could already see the writing on the wall. But, I elected to keep painting over it.

Until...I realized that time was just passing me away. After realizing that yet another year had passed, and nothing has gotten better, I became determined to make my exit. There was no hope left. No light at the end of the tunnel. No nothing to hold on to. So, I asked for a separation...told him I was going to find an apartment. He thought it would be best if he left; that way, the kids can remain in their home and schools, etc.

"Ok", I agreed.

A couple of months go by...with him out of the house (staying with his mom). Feeling a little free, I started testing the waters...but, unfortunately, didn't find much...at that particular time.

After having daily telephone conversations, he had convinced me that not only had he changed, but that he had found God. He was going to church every Sunday, and had promised that he was going to do better, be better, and that our marriage was going to improve and be stronger...if I just let him come back.

So, I did.

He had found God alright. So much so that I was being preached to every chance he got, as if I wasn't already aware of who God was. But, in addition to the preaching, I had stones being thrown at me from every direction.

I wasn't fasting right (chewing gum was never allowed). I wasn't supposed to listen to secular or worldly music – nope, not even Luther

Vandross (because it promoted sinful thoughts and actions). I wasn't supposed to entertain guests and/or family in our home who smoked and/or drank (because they would bring in devilish spirits). I shouldn't be going to a church where the pastor kept it real in the pulpit (as if his and all other pastors were free of sin). We could no longer please each other in ways that I thought we both liked, because it would make our bed defiled. I'm sorry, but were we not still married? Why would God prohibit acts between married couples that were pleasing to their spouses?

The only way he could communicate with me was through the Bible. No more, "honey, how was your day? Do you want to go to a movie tonight? Do you want to have sex tonight?" Now it's just a "hey, what do you think about this scripture? Or that scripture?"

I know. I blinked somewhere. There was something that I missed...or, that I *was* missing.

God, what now? I've got a man telling me on a daily basis that he's "saved, sanctified and filled with the Holy Ghost." I found it funny how he felt he had to keep saying it, though. It must have been his way of convincing himself...cause proof, for me, would be in your actions.

As a mother who didn't believe in sparing the rod, I was somehow always looked at as the bad guy. I would get onto our son for something or another – something worthy, of course – and he would run crying to his daddy...who said nothing in agreement with me; but instead, who elected to baby him, and make statements like, "it's ok...mommy's mean...but, I'm your friend." But, when he wants to discipline our son, I'm supposed to support *him*?

Or, how about the time when my ex-husband thought having our son reenact 'having being touched by the Holy Spirit' was funny and great. I was disgraced. I was appalled. The nerve of him allowing our son to mock a spiritual force...when, to my son, it was nothing more than freedom to jump and run around the church freely, without any repercussions. I angrily told my son to stop, only to be followed up with a disagreement by my ex-husband. Again, I was the bad guy. And, after hearing my own child tell me he wishes I would die (after disciplining him), and seeing him run – again – to his father, it was enough to make me break down.

I finally came to the conclusion that things were not getting better. Our issues had gone from bad to worse.

So, one night, I had another long talk with God. A very tearful talk. A very heart-felt talk. This was it. I was giving up. I was tired. I was through. I couldn't take it or do it anymore. "I'm outta here, Lord. For real, this time." And, all I remember asking for was His mercy, His forgiveness, and His guidance.

The next day, I told my ex-husband I was leaving, and that I would be filing for a divorce (not separation). He immediately jumped up claiming that I wasn't a Christian, and that divorce was not an option. But, more funny than that was his statement that "God would never forgive" me.

Did he not realize that judging me (as in to call me a non-Christian) was not Christian-like either? All Christians know that only One has the power and authority to judge people...and that was God.

But, ok...fine. Call me what you want to. Say what you want to. I'm still leaving.

So, to my lawyer's office I went. $1,800 to draw up my divorce papers. $25 to have them served. Now, y'all, it was never my intention to stick it to my ex-husband. The lawyer wanted to make him pay the maximum amount of child support; I pleaded with her to choose the minimum. I even said I would let him have the house with all of the furniture, and that I would continue to pay his utilities until our divorce was final (just so he couldn't say I abandoned him). And I held on to my end of the bargain, even though he never once held on to his (I have yet to receive one full child support payment).

Now, tell me I wasn't good to him? Yeah, I left him. But, it's not like he didn't know it was coming. I'd been telling him for 10 years. He never wanted to go to counseling. He never tried to do the things to make things right. And, now, because he is saved and I'm saved, he thinks we're supposed to stay together. Not this time.

I am a true believer (and witness) that when a woman's fed up, there is nothing else that can be done to get her to change her mind about leaving you. Absolutely nothing.

I Thought...

I thought when you approached me,
it would be a beautiful love affair...
I thought when you proposed,
I would no longer have a care...
I thought when we met down the aisle,
all my dreams would come true...
But, I obviously thought wrong...
cause none of these were ever proven.

I thought when we made love,
pleasures would be great and plentiful...
I thought even if we argued,
all would be forgiven through our love.
I thought my trust would increase,
and that you'd always be the one...
But, I obviously thought wrong...
cause our relationship ran its course.

I thought you would appreciate
the value in which I brought to you...
I thought you would love the complement
of me standing next to you...
I thought you could handle my success
as a token of our growth...
But, I obviously thought wrong...
cause you hated me doing more.

I thought us having a child
would bring us closer as a couple...
I thought losing weight would give
you the sexiness you were wanting...

I thought my constant drive
would bring you pleasures untold of...
But, I obviously thought wrong...
cause my worth was quickly lowered.

I thought when you came back,
all would be better cause we had God.
I thought that you would one day talk to me
as if I was still your wife.
I thought you would see how badly
you were hurting our relationship...
But, I obviously thought wrong...
cause you did nothing to stop it.

I thought a lot of things but I was
proven to have thought wrong...
Guess I didn't really know you
as well as I had thought.

Recoil...

It was supposed to be a union. But, how many of you know that if God didn't put it together, it's not going to last? No matter how hard you try. Or, how bad you want to make it work. It's just not going to last.

You have read only a few of the incidents that happened over the course of my marriage. There were countless occasions when I would have my heart pierced, my back stabbed, my mind toyed with, my body used...but, what hurt most was the fact that my spirit was wounded...beyond repair. I was no longer that outgoing woman who loved the shoes she walked in. I was no longer the loving wife I'd tried so hard to be. I was no longer strong enough to handle all of the crap that came my way. I was no longer capable of holding my feelings in. I was no longer able to smile...genuinely. I was no longer...me.

For years, I had given it my all. For years, I had tried to be a good wife, and to show him all the pleasures that life could possibly hold. For years.

All I ever asked for was proof that I was appreciated...proof that I was valued...proof that I was loved. But, instead, what I received was a feeling that I was merely nothing more than another one of his many trophies left sitting on a shelf...collecting dust. I was often angered when thinking of what my life could have been like had I taken the other road. But, like most men when traveling lost, I knew where I was going.

Not!

A relationship with no foundation is bound to crumble...just like a house with no foundation would. But, I didn't see that in the beginning. I actually thought we had a solid relationship...until years later when I finally saw the light.

Our relationship was based upon sex. From our first so-called date, sex played a part. Every time we saw each other afterwards, sex was somewhere in the picture. Conversations with substance... expressions of true feelings...dates that allowed us to explore our likes and dislikes...opportunities to reveal true personalities... opportunities to expose true intentions...were all few and far between.

We didn't know each other. We thought we did; but we didn't. We weren't ready for marriage. We weren't ready for a child together. We weren't ready for all of life's trials and tribulations. We weren't strong enough to handle them. After all, the foundation we were standing on had nothing to do with God. Just dirt and wood. Nothing concrete to hold us. Nothing framed to sustain us. *Our* house would be the one the Big Bad Wolf would puff once on and it fall completely apart.

I used to always wonder if I was destined to fail. Only three women in my entire family have I even seen stay married to their spouses...all others were quick to let go. I used to always say that my insatiable ways would prevent me from staying in my marriage. I was always replacing things when I got tired of them, when I got bored with them, when I wanted or needed something new. If I wanted a new car, I got it. When I wanted new clothes, I got them. When I wanted a new house, I got it. My ex-husband used to always joke that I would replace him, too. Let this be a lesson to those who don't believe...be very careful what you speak out of your mouth. As the Bible clearly states, your tongue has a lot of power...and what you speak from it can actually come true...and very often does.

I can honestly admit that on the day of my marriage, I wasn't very happy. As I told you earlier, I was already hearing my spirit and it's "no" warnings. But, I just knew that things could change. I was a believer in what could, instead of being understanding of what wasn't. I wanted to be married so badly that I was willing to risk my livelihood. I thought I would gain a sense of security, and someone who would be with me for the rest of my life.

But, after nervously walking down the aisle, I began realizing that I was already dying...inside. I wasn't in love with this man. I didn't even like this man. All I've ever encountered with him was pain, pain, and more pain. Nothing was right. Nothing even felt right. The look in his eyes as I was approaching him wasn't even right. The vows that I was repeating were so distant in thought that I couldn't begin to tell you all of what was said. I was hurting right there. I was dying right there. I had every opportunity to call it off...but, I froze.

From that day forward, it has taken all I had to survive. I thought the chapter that I entitled, 'Wronged', would have been my hardest...but, I actually think – now – that this one is. Only because I can still feel the pain...buried deep. Even though I have left, gotten divorced, moved on, and forgiven him, I'm still hurting.

Ten plus years is a long time to deal with things that tore at your very being. No, I wasn't physically abused. But, I was...emotionally. And, the funny part of it all is that I don't even think he meant it, or knows it. He's probably still unsure as to why I left. In his mind, I bet he thinks that nothing was *that* bad...and there was nothing that we could not have worked out...with God on our sides. And, that last statement may very well be true. With God on our sides, we could have accomplished something. But, I was too wounded to even try.

I cried so hard when I had to tell God I was leaving my marriage. Mostly because I had read every scripture in the Bible that referenced anything about divorce, and I knew God hated divorce. But, I also read, believed and knew that God was a forgiving God...that He was an understanding God...that He was a merciful God...and, most of all, that He was a loving God.

I knew that there would be consequences that I would have to endure, like money being tight, kids being angry, families being torn, hearts being hard to heal, relationships being hard to maintain; but, I heard this voice one day saying, "through it all, you will survive...if you just stand, hold onto my hand, and press through, I will give you the strength you need. I will give you the courage you need. I will give you all that you need...if you can just keep the faith...if you can just believe in Me."

Just repeating those words on this page brings tears to my eyes, because I was touched by them. I'm being healed by them. I'm being led by them. I'm being sustained by them. I'm being reformed by them. God is truly an awesome God. A faithful God. A true and living God. I am, indeed, a witness. And, I am, indeed, His child.

For those of you who have been happily married for years and years, my hat goes off to you! I solute you for being able to maintain...for being able to hold on, despite the rough times...for being able to keep on, regardless of the stormy times...to live on, just because there are times. You are my heroes...and, through your testimonies, I have hope. Congratulations...and God bless!

But, for those of you who are going through turmoil in your marriages, my only advice to you is to seek God. For those of you who are confused and don't know where else to turn, seek God. For those of you who are at your wits end and can't see yourself taking another step, please seek God. Talk to Him. He already knows your struggles. He already knows your pains. He just needs you to seek Him. To call on Him. To rely on Him. To trust in Him. To believe in Him.

If He could bring me through it, He could bring you, as well.

Now, I'm not an advocate for divorce. I do believe you should try to do all you can do to make your marriage work. But, I don't believe you should lose yourself in the process. I don't believe that you should be forced to stay in something that is not spiritually fulfilling, emotionally fulfilling or physically fulfilling. I don't believe you should ever stay if being physically abused. Trying to make things work when being tortured with violence is never an option!

To those of you who are not sure if you and your spouse are going to make it another month, let alone another year, it is your marital duty to communicate, to listen, to try your hardest to turn things around...and the best way to do that is to pray...together. You know they always say 'a family that prays together stays together.' That is not a lie...but, you've got to start praying before things start going downhill...before things start getting bad.

Get yourselves acquainted with God early. Ask Him to always cover your marriage, protect your marriage, and to rebuke evil forces when you and/or your spouse are too weak to. Ask Him to strengthen you as a couple, to unite and line up not only your minds and hearts, but also your spirits. And, should you have gotten married (without the presence of God anywhere in your daily lives), pray that He forms a bond between the two of you that no other man [or woman] can tear apart. Ask Him to bless your marriage, to bless your family, and to always give you the mindset and means to care for one another, to cherish one another, and to always love one another.

If your spouse comes to you with an issue, always, always take time to listen. But, don't just stop there; that's only half the battle. The other half is to compromise and sacrifice. If the issue is something that can be rectified by a tweaking of an attitude, an adjustment of a mindset, a showing of affection, just do it. That's only a small price to pay to keep your marriage rolling. But, if the issue involves doing something that causes conflict, that is morally wrong, or spiritually depriving, you've got to come back with some heavy artillery. Something that can leave a mark...for life. That something is called, the 'Word.' When you've tried all you can try, said all you can say, done all you can do...seek God's Word. No matter your religion, reference God's Word. Read. Comprehend. Study. Apply. Wait. Listen. Do.

And, if getting divorced is still on the brain, please don't think for once that it will be easy. As I prefaced this chapter, and have stated in other chapters, there is always a consequence...to every action that you take.

There will always be repercussions...some good, some bad...but, that's why it always best to seek God first. He has your best interest at heart. He can protect you. He can guide you. He can make ways out of no ways. He can do the unthinkable.

He is, after all, God. The Almighty. The All Powerful. Lord of all Lords. King of all Kings. Maker of Heaven and Earth. Maker of *you*. There's no one more powerful. There's no one more faithful. There's no one more loving.

If your spouse doesn't take the time to love you, to cherish you, to edify and support you...you will want to have that talk. If your spouse takes you for granted, neglects your needs, and only thinks of themselves...you will want to have that talk. If you are being physically abused...emotionally abused...or spiritually abused...you will want to have that talk. If you're finding out on a daily basis that you and your spouse are unequally yoked...you will want to have that talk. If your spouse doesn't listen, blames you and takes no responsibility for their share of the problems in your marriage...you will want to have that talk. If your spouse doesn't submit to, complement or care for you...you will want to have that talk. If your spouse is abusing, neglecting or tormenting your kids...you will want to have that talk. If your spouse is causing you to be mentally depressed, causing you to spiritually regress, or causing pain in your chest...you will want to have that talk.
You will want to have that talk...with the only counselor qualified to listen, the only attorney qualified to fight for you, and the only judge qualified to grant you victory...His name is God.

As the lover of your soul, He should be your first love...your first priority. If your relationship with Him isn't right, your relationship with your spouse will not be right. God is a jealous God; and, as mentioned before, He and only He has that right to be. It is important that you understand the order in which to live...God's order.

God is always first. Your morning hellos, your evening goodnights, your desires to talk to someone, your need to love someone, your thought to thank someone...should all be first made towards God. No other man, woman, child, job, or animal could ever take the place of God...could ever love you as much as God does...would be there for you longer than God can.

Think about it...when your spouse or love ones leave this earth...when your pet dies...when you lose or leave your job...there is only one constant left...God. Why wouldn't you put Him first? He is eternal...His love is everlasting...and His mercy and grace endures forever. When others turn their back on you, deceive you, hurt you, manipulate and/or take advantage of you, God is still there...still faithful...still loving...still waiting...for you to see that only He can supply all of your needs, and is completely able to be your everything.

Second to God, in the order of things, would be your spouse. I know, you feel your children should come next...after all, they are your direct bloodline, a product of your seed, your fruit, and so on...but, that's not God's order. Your spouse comes second. And, when I say spouse, I mean your legally abiding husband or wife...not your live-in partner, your long-time-might-as-well-be-married partner, but, your wedded spouse. That person should be next on your priority list to submit to and take care of, to edify and to love. Whatever needs they have – as long as they are morally and spiritually in-line with God's Will – should be considered and/or fulfilled.

Spouses come second because when you marry someone, you are committing to spend the rest of your life with that person. Your children will grow up, leave the home, and eventually start their own families. And, if you live your life putting your children before your spouse, you and your spouse's relationship may be in jeopardy once your children finally do leave the nest (if not before). For this reason, your spouse comes second...children come third...extended family and friends come fourth...and you, my friend, unselfishly come last.

That is God's order. Love Him...first. Place Him...first. See that you are living to please Him...first. If you can commit to doing this, not only will your relationship with Him get and be stronger; but, He will be more merciful to giving you, His bridesmaid, the desires of your heart.

Now, that's not to say that you will not go through things. You will always go through things...whether married or just in a relationship. But, your success in those situations depends greatly on your relationship with God, along with how you choose to handle the trials that are being thrown your way. You can cry about it. You can whine about it. You can beat your spouse until they're blue and purple. Or, you can choose to let your first love handle that battle for you.

People still ask me today, seeing how I've been going through some really rough times since my divorce, if I regretted my decision to leave? My answer now, as it was then, is still, "No. I have no regrets."

While being married, I noticed that the only time I made myself pray was when I was nearing my breaking point. When my livelihood was being jeopardized. When my spirit was being broken. When my esteem was being lowered. When my thoughts were being conflicted. When my body was left craving. When his lies were beginning to surface. When my eyes were starting to roam. When my marriage was becoming an afterthought instead of a forethought. When my motherhood was being shaken. When my spirituality was being questioned. When my knowledge of God and His ways were being tested.

The evil one was truly working. And, I do mean working. Succeeding at most turns. Winning at most battles. But, you know what? I don't consider it a complete success...cause he did nothing to stop God's mission.

Staying in that marriage would have drained me...destroyed me...killed me. But, I've got life...now. From having to go through the things I went through in my marriage, and then going through the things I have since my divorce, I've managed to develop and strengthen my belief and faith in God. I now have a beautiful and lasting relationship with my God, my Savior, my Father, my King, my Redeemer, my Provider, my Protector, my Healer, my Miracle Maker, my Groom, my Everything. My *absolute* everything.

There may come a point in your life when you have to decide which direction to proceed in...which road to go down...which option is best for you to take. With regards to my marriage, I'd like to think that all things happened for a reason.

There was a reason I got married. And, there was also a reason I got divorced.

Thank you, God.

ROUND FIVE:
H8ERS

Never was super cute,
but you couldn't tell from the hatred.
Ever since I was a youngster,
I've always had around me fakesters.
From family members who became jealous
at the luxuries I would get...
To so-called friends around the way
who never intended to have my back.
Funny how people always say
they wish you the best, but really don't.
Or, how if someone goes to help,
they always expect double in return.
No issues with the opposite sex,
unless we're speaking about perversion.
But, the women (around my age)...
their issues extended further.
Could be walking down the hallways
of my school, church or job.
Would smile and sincerely say, hello,
but, in return I get snubbed.
Like I was the one in the wrong;
perhaps, I should have never spoke.
I just laugh now-a-days,
cause on their hatred, they will choke.
I'm "not friendly or approachable"...

I've heard many a reasons why.
I "think I'm better than everyone else"...
all – crazy, crazy lies.
Intimidation is my aurora
to those who can only see one side.
Sometimes it takes a little effort,
if you want to ride this ride.
Guarded up, yes, I stay;
but, that's no reason for alarm.
I'm as harmless as a fly,
unless you succeed in pissing me off.
My biggest issue has always been
women who felt the need to compete.
What they fail to realize is
that they are them, and I am me.
Being a show-off is not in my character;
but, I do try to have a good time.
Just found it funny how I was always
the one labeled as the blame.
For being the seducer or the flirt
who caused their men's eyes to roam.
Like I honestly had a desire
to break up a happy home.
Just because he might be cute
doesn't mean I want to taste his flavor.
I'm very stingy with my indulgences...
if he ain't free, I ain't craving.
Still I manage to get those looks,

whenever I walk into a room.
They say that I command attention
by the confidence that I show.
Wasn't liked by the town's women,
cause at 21, I was expressing myself.
Befriended someone's husband...
they were separated, so, I didn't care.
Never liked her anyway,
she played crazy, but I was there.
If only she had gotten out,
them .22's would have quickly spread.
Often wanted to show that side,
to continue on with my father's legacy.
Cause "see tho, what it is tho...
I wanted to rent, buy, then pawn" her.
I'm not that way anymore, though...
I thank God for my growth.
I treat others as I wish to be;
I keep moving to not be broken.
Every day, it's a different story...
Some people like me, and some don't.
But, as Katt Williams once suggested,
"let your haters do their jobs."
So, now I've learned to turn a cheek,
and do it moving for all that fail
to recognize and realize that
gaining their friendship is not a care.
So sick of people pretending to be

what they're not and will never be...
Forever talking behind your back;
but in your face, always grinning.
I will admit to being tempted,
as the evil one truly has a way...
of creeping upon my senses,
making these cat hairs stand up straight.
Had so-called neighbors who insisted
that they were true and real friends.
Only to find out I was better off
not associating with snakes like them.
Either they're trying to take your man,
or trying to use you for everything.
"Can I borrow? Will you take me?
What size clothes do you wear?"
I've heard it all. I've seen it all,
and ain't trying to keep going back.
I truly hate dealing with people
whose goal is to bring strife into my life.
Although I know they'll always be there,
I have to pray for their quick removal.
Cause God knows what I can deal with,
and just how much I can handle.

...If God be for us, who can be against us?

Romans 8:31 (KJV)

I see you.

I know you see me.

I hear you.

I know you hear me.

I know you.

I know you *think* you know me.

But, in reality...you don't. You don't know me. You have no idea who I am. Or, what I stand for.

You look at me and roll your eyes. You watch me and get disgusted. You hear words coming from my mouth, and immediately get all choked up. You don't like me. You can't stand me. You wish I didn't exist.

But, I do...I still do.

Over forty years in the making...and I am still trying to figure out just what it is that makes one hate on me. Perhaps it's the perfume I'm wearing that makes them turn their noses up. And, maybe, their eyes roll in another direction because my clothing is not to their liking. Or, perhaps my voice is too soft for them to hear me speak, as they continue to just pass me by.

I could literally be walking down the hallways of my school, job, church, etc., sincerely saying hello and smiling at a woman coming in my direction...and, 90% of the time, that woman would look the other way and/or pretend that I didn't even exist – especially if she's around my age. No 'hello' back, no smile, no acknowledgment whatsoever. And, if there was an acknowledgement, it was a rolled eye. What?! What did I do to her? Besides speak? Nicely?

I could probably be a millionaire right now if I had a dime for every time I've been disregarded and/or treated as if I didn't exist in the same room, on the same hallway, or even in the same elevator as another. And, honestly speaking, I could probably still become a millionaire even if I were to start collecting right now.

One would think that – by now – I would no longer be surprised at the level of jealousy and hatred that is still being projected towards me – based upon my possessions, my career status, the color of my skin, the bow in my legs, the confidence in my walk and/or speech, or whatever else one could think of to hate on me for.

As a child, I had cousins who were jealous of me because "I could get anything I wanted" ...because "I never got into trouble"...because it seemed as if "our elders loved me more." But, in reality, that was not the case at all.

As an adult, I've found family members and so-called friends who, I can tell, are, still jealous of me. And I still have to wonder just why that is. Maybe, it's because...God has blessed me with beauty that I don't have to make up? Or that He's blessed me with a car that I don't have to fix up? Or, perhaps it's because my kids are behaved enough that I don't have to whip up? Or, that God gives me strength when the urge comes for me to crack up? Or, maybe it's because I'm sensible enough to move on instead of tolerating those who screw up?

Whatever it is, I've found it hilariously funny that my haters would rather spend their time hating on me than bettering themselves...than making a life for themselves...than doing the things that will make themselves happy? All of that energy being used...on the wrong person, in the wrong way at the wrong times.

To this day, I am able to count the number of friends (who have been true friends to me) on less than one hand...meaning, there's been less than five. Yes, you read that correctly...in over 40 years, I've had less than five 'truly down for me' friends.

Now, perhaps that's because I – since a young child – have tried to disassociate myself with fake and/or phony people. You know... those people who would smile in your face and talk behind your back...those people who would pretend to be on your side, but stab you in it every opportunity they got...those people who try to prevent your success and/or advancement, just so they can continue deceiving others (and themselves) into thinking they're better than you.

I've had so-called friends who've tried to say or do things to undermine everything I put into motion. If I was excelling in my career, I had folks trying to convince others that I wasn't doing a good job...that I wasn't worthy of my position...that I didn't deserve to make as much money as I did...that I must have gotten where I was because some manager was attracted to and/or doing me.

Why couldn't it just be that I have skills? Initiative? Drive? Passion? And an uncharted ability to learn and/or perform any job placed before me? Why couldn't I just be a smart, dedicated and reliable worker?

Why does something always have to be wrong with me, in order for someone to feel good about themselves? Why does someone always have to turn my positives into negatives, just so they can appear more worthy? Where does all of that come from?

I can't recall one time in which I have ever intentionally tried to hurt someone's feelings. Not one time had I ever picked a fight, or called someone out of their name, or even wished something bad upon someone (aside from those who wronged me). Not one time have I ever looked down on someone who may have appeared to be less fortunate than I, and didn't try to help in some way. I have always been the generous, thoughtful and caring one...have always treated others as I, myself, would have wanted to be treated...and, as mentioned in a previous chapter...have always shown love. But, all of the hatred that I've received from others has truly made me lose respect for certain types of individuals...particularly those who scheme, lie, and back-stab.

Have you ever had a same-sex friend who was always trying to be around you...who was always wanting to hang around you...who always wanted to do what you did...look like you did...act like you did...talk how you did...walk like you did...or, get what you got?

Or, how about that friend who was always thanking you for being there for them, and who insisted that they valued your friendship...who tried their best to make you believe that they would be there for you, always having your back...who was always willing to listen to your problems – especially if they involved issues with your man, job, family, etc.?

Or, how about those who swear they wouldn't know what they would do without you...if you were not there to help them through this trial or that issue...if you didn't come through for them in this situation or the last...who swore they were independent and could handle theirs; yet, you found them always coming to you for something – either to borrow this, to use that, to watch them, or to buy those?

There comes a point in those so-called 'friendships' that you have to sit back and truly analyze what's really happening.

In my life, I've had all of these types of people around me...but, thankfully, God shielded me from being completely taken. You see, although I appeared to be friendly, I've always managed to keep a distance. And, it was that distance that allowed me to see just what type of person those so-called friends were.

It goes like this...if you're too close to an ingenuous person, or if you allow a deceptive person to get too close to you, you can sometimes become blinded to their tactics – similar to that of a blind spot in your car: you can't always rely on the positioning of your mirrors to tell the whole story...sometimes, you have to look over your shoulders to see the entire view.

I find myself giving advice to so many people with regards to their relationships with others...especially those of the same sex. Some sit back and say their friends aren't like 'that' and would never do 'that', etc., etc....only to find out shortly down the road that that friend did the very act that they insisted they wouldn't do.

What one has to remember is that people are fare-weather and peculiar individuals. Some are genuine. Most are fake. Some have your best interest at heart. Most just want to use and abuse you, and/or secretly destroy you and/or your relationships.

You've heard of the old saying, 'keep your enemies close'...well, my experiences have all lead me to keeping my so-called friends closer. Only because...that best girlfriend who you tell *everything* to...that girlfriend who knows *all* about you and your man...how good your man is, how bad your man is...what your man did for you last week...how your man made you feel in bed the other night...*that* girlfriend – you better be watching.

I always advise people to keep their personal lives personal. Absolutely no one should know what goes on under your roof, and definitely not what goes on behind your bedroom doors. The more you talk, the more you invite trouble...especially if you're associating yourself with under-cover haters.

As soon as a hater sees you slipping, turning your back, or no longer looking...as soon as they have gotten you to trust them and let your guard down...their plan is put into motion.

My advice....do whatever you can to protect yourself.

Keep people out of your business...out of your homes...out of your relationships. Protect those you hold dear...especially your mates. I say this because the biggest form of hatred I've seen is the hatred over successful relationships.

What may appear to be an innocent flirt, or an apparent dislike (by your 'friend' over your mate) could very well turn into a situation that'll have you wanting to kill someone. If your friend doesn't have a mate, and/or if they're not content in their own relationship, your relationship can very well become a target.

"Why should she be happy, if I'm not?" "Why can't I get what she's getting? I can love and treat him so much better."

These are the words that are being secretly spoken behind your back. And, trust me when I say, statements like these are being thought, said and reacted upon...on a daily basis. So, do not – by any means – think that *your* friend is innocent. Do not – by any means – think that your mate will always be strong enough to handle temptations being thrown their way.

Since the beginning of time, starting with Adam and Eve, we've seen where a hater (Satan, in this case) can provoke and/or cause complete destruction. It has been proven that haters (men and women) can have very conniving ways of getting what they want...especially if they have a convincing tongue and/or sex appeal. So, you have to be very careful with that can you open...because, what you thought was going to be a tasteful can of peaches could very well turn into a gut-turning can of worms.

As I've noted before, people are fleshly, carnal-minded individuals who can very easily be tempted into doing the wrong thing...mostly due to them being spiritually and morally faulty. You can see these faults on television every day...you can witness those faults being acted out in movies all the time...you can read about those faults in countless books and magazines...you can even hear stories about those faults from persons you would least suspect.

With that being said, you can either be attentive and heed the warnings, or you can keep living foolishly – thinking that all is well in your camp.

For those of you who are sitting back thinking that you and your relationship are exempt, I truly feel sorry for you. You and your mate can have all of the faith in the world...you may even think that your mate is so spiritually grounded that nothing and no one can come between you...but, I am here to tell you that even preachers fall prey to fleshly temptations. The only thing you can hold on to is your hope that God will keep you and your mate on a straight and narrow path...and that your love for each other (and God) will surpass those temptations.

Now, don't get me wrong...I'm not saying that *all* relationships are in trouble...or that *all* friends are deceitful and conniving...or that *all* mates will fall weak to temptation. Nor, am I saying that you shouldn't trust your closest friends and/or mates. I am simply saying that you should not be fooled into thinking that you won't be dealt some unwanted cards in life by unsuspecting persons within your very own circle.

Always remember that not everyone who smiles in your face is your friend. With this being said, it would just be in your best interest to always pay attention to your surroundings...to keep a watchful eye and a listening ear to *every* thing.

Now, some of you may be asking, just what does all of what I just said have to do with 'hating.' Absolutely *everything*! Some people can see when *you're* happy, some people can see the amount of attention *you* get, some people can see *your* successes, some people can see how things always seem to be going *your* way. These sights (even though those people are on the outside looking in) can appear to be glorious...provoking envy in some that are around you. Envy, in turn, provokes insecurities...insecurities, in turn, provokes jealousy...jealousy, in turn, provokes hatred.

Now, there are many ways in which a person can show that they are hating on you...that they really don't like you...that they are truly not for you...and trying to take what is yours and/or trying to steal your joy is the grandest way of all.

Some people will just talk behind your back...but, some can be more direct with their hatred. Some haters can be distant (like the ones you only see on the job, or at the grocery store); while, others can be as close as in your own home (ie, your spouse, parents or kids). But, no matter where or who they are, the point remains that you – some time throughout the course of your life – will, in some way or another, have to face and/or come up against some form of hatred.
Trust me...I've lived it all of my life.

I have seen just how manipulative people can be...just how far people will go...and, just how much destruction people can cause. And, I shall not sit here and say that I haven't been bothered at times. I won't even sit here and lie about me never having been affected - in some way. But, what I will do is admit to you that with each experience, I've been made stronger...stronger because I now realize and understand what those people around me were doing...

Hating.

Hate On Me

Could it be my walk?
Or, is it the thickness of my hips?
Or, is it the way your man stares
at the way my dress fits?
The long bow legs that I have?
The country girl accent that I speak?
Just what is it that makes you
have to really hate on me?
Am I the one your boyfriend thinks of
when you're getting on his nerves?
Or, am I that office distraction
that pulled them away from your cube?
Could it be that I'm not like you...
that I have a rather tasteful flavor?
Or, that all are comfortable
around my sweet and pleasant nature?
Maybe it's the way I work the crowd
whenever I enter into the place.
Or, the way I smile at you
when I know behind my back you speak?
Maybe it's because I'm favored
when you think I shouldn't be?
Or, cause God's given me a nice crib,
car, and two wonderful kids?
Maybe it's because doors got opened
and opportunities were presented?
What exactly bothers you?
What have I done to be resented?
It really saddens me to know
that I've become a thorn in your side.

Cause, the funny part about it all
is that I wasn't even trying.
I really wish I could help you
get past and over your hater-hood.
Cause all that stress you're causing yourself
does you very little good.
I know it's hard when your securities
become threatened in some way.
But, what you fail to realize is
that I'm not the one you need to hate.
You have to know that in spite of your thoughts,
I'm still going to be me.
You'd rather worry about the unchangeable;
I prefer to be worry-free.
But, go ahead, if it pleases you...
I dare not stop you from doing you.
Just think there's a plethora of other things
you could set your mind to.
Whether it be today, tomorrow,
or any of the following days ...
I won't stress over your hating...
cause, your attention, I appreciate.

Recoil...

Envy...Insecurity...Jealousy...Hatred.

So, what if that girl or guy is more attractive than you? So what if their outfit is more on point than yours? And, who cares about the flowers or expressions of love their mate had delivered to them last Friday...and the Friday before that? They may have children on the Honor Roll. You may have even watched them get that promotion you've been working so hard to obtain. But, none of these things would justify the spending of your time and/or energy hating on them.

Have you ever noticed someone of the same sex who was just drop dead gorgeous? To the point that you find yourself saying, "wow, I wish my stomach was as flat as hers...or my hair was as pretty as hers...or my clothes fit as nice as his?" Well, guess what? You may have been hating.

Or, how about that new girl on the job? Have you taken notice to how all the guys are flocking around her? How she tends to have this silly, innocent, Betty Boop girlie smile on her face every time guys talk to her? Or, have you noticed yourself smirking as she switched her hips in that too short of a mini-skirt that has all of the guys whistling under their breaths? Then, yes...again...you may have been hating.

How about the Jones' next door? Have you ever admired your neighbor's home or household possessions? Or, how clean and sleek their brand new German import is? To the point that, perhaps, you found yourself asking just how they could afford that much house or car anyway? "Somebody must be selling drugs or something." If you said those words, you may have, again, been hating.

Face it. We all have a little hatred in us. But, it's what we do with that hatred that determines the level of our "hater-hood". You see, in my book, there are degrees of hater-hood: first, second and third.

First degree hater-hood is for the "innocent, one-thought, wish-game" haters. Yeah, you thought they were cute, their hair was fly, their outfit was on point; but, soon after you say that, the 'wish' game starts… "Wished my hair looked like…wished I could get my clothes to fit like…wished I could afford to get or buy that…" But, be careful…cause too many of those wishes can result in you reaching hater-hood in the second degree.

Second degree hater-hood is that "was innocent, one thought, wished I was like…" hatred that tends to linger…provoking repeated thoughts of that person every time you see them. You may find yourself making little comments about that person here and there that won't necessarily be in a positive light.

"She's cute, but she's not all that…her waist is small, but it could be smaller…his project was good, but it could have been better…" All of which will ultimately lead you to the next degree.

Third degree is that level of hater-hood where you always have something negative to say about a particular person(s)…where you find yourself talking down or badly about them to others, just so you can somehow seem superior to them…like now, there's nothing this person can wear that is appealing or up to your standards…like now, that person's home looks run down compared to the house you don't have, but can get…like now, everything they do, you can all-of-a-sudden do better…knowing good and well, the tables haven't turned. You still look the same way you did…and have the same things you did…and so do they. So, stop it! Don't do yourself like that!

What does that person have that you can't get? Nowadays, you can have anything you want (with a little money and know-how). If you got small breasts or buttocks, you can get implants added. If you want a flat stomach, you can get a liposuction. If you can't find a date for that important function, you can hire an escort. If you're driving that can't-

pass-emissions car, you can buy, lease or rent a newer model. If you're living in a 40-year-old house, you can upgrade to a newer one.
Or, ok...perhaps, realistically, those things aren't so readily available for you to obtain, especially if you've let your credit get bad or your income can't really support the purchase; but, the thing you MUST remember in your times of first, second or third-degree hatred is that God made each of us individually, purposed with our own missions...meaning, our paths will be different, our likes and dislikes will be different, our circumstances will be different, and our needs will be different...which all play a role in our blessings being different.

Those persons you are hating on may appear to have nicer things or look better, etc.; but, you never know what they had to do or go through to get those things.

As for those beautiful, six-pack-stomach-having people you often compare yourself to, forget about them. Cause you see, what you don't know is that she had to have a rib taken out of her side to get her abs to look like that; and, as a result, she's left – two years later – feeling pains where the incisions were. And, as for that guy's silky smooth, razor-bump-free face, he had to have plastic surgery to get his face to look like that; but, if you look closely, you can see where the laser beams have actually began eating away at his skin. And, yeah, her husband may be so, so attractive and appear to be the ideal man; but, what she ain't telling you is how he beats on her every night. And, yeah, they might have a nice house and other material things...but, they can't buy anything else because they've completely charged up their credit cards, used all of their savings, and are now facing bankruptcy.

Now, I know those things may be a bit on the extreme side...but, the point I'm trying to get you to see is that not everything is what it's cracked up to be. Not everyone is who they appear to be. The prettiest girl can be the ugliest girl, because her attitude stinks. The most powerful woman on your job may appear to have all she wants, but she can't have children. The finest house could be the worst house, because the foundation is cracking and all of the plumbing is bad. The richest of the rich could seem to be happy; but, in reality, be the most unhappy, because they are lacking love, which money can't buy.

All of these things are why I say, stop focusing and worrying about other people and their possessions. And, instead, choose to love and focus on you and the things you have...choose to accept your circumstances...and be comfortable in your surroundings.

Know that you are attractive...that you are important...that you are significant... that you are loved...despite whatever imperfections and/or flaws you *think* you may have. You may very well be unattractive to most...but, if God made you with a loving spirit, you, my friend, are the most beautiful person in the world. Because when all the beauty is gone from the pretty ones, if their spirits were ugly, people won't like them for long anyway. But, you and your beautiful spirit will shine far longer, because that's what really matters most.

So, love yourself...for who you are...for what you got...for what you're trying to be...for where you're trying to go. Cause, nine times out of 10, those people you're hating on could probably care less about you and/or what you've got. Hence the reason why you shouldn't be worrying about them and what they've got. Life is too short to be caring about why someone has something you don't...why someone appears to be happy and you're not...why someone seems to be liked more than you. God made you just the way you are. And, there is beauty within you. There is strength and courage within you. There is love within you.

And, if you're saying you have yet to see it, then that's what you need to spend your time focusing on...finding and loving you...instead of hating on others. You should take some time out to pray, instead. Turn your head and heart towards the mountain from which all of your blessings fall from...place God first, and all of the other mess you're focusing on will be silly thoughts of your past. God will uplift you...encourage you...and take you to greater heights. He said He will even give you the desires of your heart, if you place Him first.

So, try Him...the next time you have a craving to hate on someone, ask God to move in you...and let you see the beauty and the blessings that *you* possess. And, stop judging a book by its cover. Not everything that glitters is gold. Not everything that sparkles is legit. Open the book, read the contents and the depth of the story will be revealed to you.

Me...I am who I am. I am in no way perfect. I am in no way where I need to be. But, I'm thankful for the mercy and favor that God has continued to show me over the years. I have been blessed...but, my blessings didn't come easy.

Some of the things that I've had to endure to get what I have were not pretty or in any way liked. Some roads I've had to travel to get where I am have not all been smooth or straight. So, to my haters who think I was dealt life on a silver platter, think again. As I mentioned, you don't know me.

Just because I can cover my pain and anguish with a smile doesn't mean I haven't gone through anything; I could be a great pretender. And, just because my swagger seems as if I can get any man I want doesn't mean that it's actually true; I may have insecurities that block all of that.

I don't and have never looked at myself as being better than the next person; nor do I look at myself as being any worse. But, what I do know is that I am and can be a good person...a loyal friend to those who can prove to be one back, a loving mate to those who can prove to love back, a faithful worker to those who can appreciate good talent. But, you won't know that if you let your hatred and/or jealousy stop you from getting to know me.

So, smile...and look at the bright side...I'm not perfect, and neither or you. I'm no better than you, and you're not better than me. God doesn't love me any more than He loves you. We are equals in this thing called life...all here for a purpose...all here to complete a mission. So, let's not defeat ourselves...but, instead love ourselves. As the scripture says, with God on our side, who can be against us?

Now, with all of that being said, there is a flip side to what I just mentioned.

I know I primarily focused on informing the haters of how to stop hating. So, let me take a moment – now – to let those who may be getting hated on know how to deal with their haters. Two and a half words..."Let'em hate!"

As one of my most favorite comedians (Katt Williams) once said, "Don't try to stop a hater from hating...Hating is a hater's job...so, let them do their jobs." They may not have been born to hate...but, they were certainly bred to hate. And, like the stellar of dogs or horses that were bred to be the best dog or horse on the track, your haters were bred to be the best haters they could be. But, unlike the dogs and horses who race...run...and win, haters can only talk... complain...and lose.

Over the years, I've actually learned to appreciate my haters. "Why?" you ask? Because the more haters I have, the more I know I'm doing something right. I get a kick out of and truly love the compliments they give when they don't look at me. I also love the sentiments they share when they don't speak to me. I even adore the laughter they present when they tell lies about me that the truth eventually discredits. It's like looking at a big, beautiful rainbow in the sky after a heavy rain storm. My haters bring me joy...in a strange but wonderful way.

So, you see, you have to learn to just smile...and keep it moving. You have to continue to do you. You have to continue to be you. You have to continue to please you. Because if you left it up to your haters, you would be in a ditch somewhere buried six feet under. God has shown you that He loves you too much to have you entertain such foolishness.

And, you (like myself) are equipped with enough self-love to not give your haters the satisfaction of knowing that they get to you.

If you have people in your life that are trying to tear you down, remove them. If you have people in your life who are interfering in your relationships, remove them. If you have people in your life who are causing you grief...on the job, at church, in the classroom...take a moment to pray for them; then, remove them...from your thoughts first...and, then, from your memory bank.

And, if you can't seem to keep them from *bothering* you, call on the only true friend who you can trust – wholeheartedly – not to *EVER* hurt, deceive or destroy you. That FRIEND is GOD.

Learn to keep your business to yourself (and God). That means...keep your lips shut. Learn to keep your relationships to yourself (and God). That means...keep your lips shut. Learn to keep your joys and your sorrows to yourself (and God). That means...keep your lips shut.

Keeping your circle small (with just you and God) enables you to decrease the amount of space available for the haters to come in. And, there not being space means there's no room to invite the pain and/or anguish that can sometimes come when you allow your haters to infiltrate.

A hater is...one who hates.
Hate is to dislike intensely or passionately.

A lover is...one who loves.
Love is to have a strong liking for, to take great pleasure in.

...and, God called us to be lovers.

So, be grateful for your haters. They, again, prove just how well-liked and admired you are.

**But I say unto you which hear, Love your
enemies, do good to them which hate you,
Bless them that curse you, and pray
for them which despitefully use you.**

Luke 6:27-28 (KJV)

ROUND SIX:
KEEPING 'EM MOVIN'

From a little girl, I've always dreamed
that girly girl's dream...
To have a knight in shining armor
climb the wall and rescue me.
Always looking for signs and wonders
from the Magnificent One above.
But was continuously disappointed
by the so-called real loves.
Heard line after line, story after story...
until I just gave up on listening.
Closed the doors and built a wall,
cause I was tired of the trickery.
Now, not many have learned to reach me,
not many even know how.
But, none have I let infiltrate
the depths of my heart.
Since the ripe age of 12,
I've fantasized about 'the one'.
The one that would take me and adore me
and forever give his love.
Thought it would have been my first crush;
then, perhaps my puppy love.
But, neither proved to be that 'one'
sent from the Heavens above.

Was introduced over the phone
to a lil' thug boy from the west side.
Like Allen Iverson after a win,
my heart was stolen by his smile.
Loved his family and thoroughly enjoyed
the nights we'd fall asleep talking.
From Adamsville to Five Points,
his love was always there to warm me.
My first orgasm was experienced
from the thrusts of this young man.
Had me wanting to spend all my days and nights
with and around him.
Taught me to shoot my first hand gun –
a white marbled .22.
Had gentle ways around me...
but, was a bad boy in his hood.
Relationship was short-lived,
because I knew I needed more.
I had a son and many goals,
and couldn't see where he was going.
So I moved on to the next...
a tall fella who was well off.
A nice young man with a sense of humor...
made me laugh at all his jokes.
He was a little on the soft side, though...
vulnerable to the cunning mind.
Never had plans to scheme;
but, I was under my cousin's advice.

"The quickest way to his money is to cry,
I'm pregnant and can't have it."
It worked, but I hated lying,
cause he did nothing to deserve it.
Wished I had confessed,
cause I was wrong to the highest degree.
He's probably somewhere still thinking
we aborted his first seed.
Relationship was short-lived;
I was being consumed with other activities.
One has got to keep it popping
if they want to successfully sustain me.
Had flings and things and actually thought
I could have any that I wanted.
My swagger was innocently charming...
my mannerisms, quite seductive.
Played the field, did my dirt,
but my heart was left craving...
For a love unlike any other,
a love that could forever hold me.
My next chance was a married man
from over the tracks, around the way.
He was gentle, sweet, and talented...
from his wife he was separated.
Hated to see the drama that
she was often putting him through.
My heart went out to him greatly...
cause he didn't deserve the abuse.

He was ten years my senior
and his experience really showed.
Well-stacked, I do remember...
can still feel the deepness of his thrusts.
And the lemon popsicle trail
that his tongue would slowly follow...
I had a wonderful time learning...
the experiences were truly awesome.
Out of all my past loves,
a soul mate he could have been.
Always knew what I was thinking,
stayed abreast of every movement.
Used to think he was the 'one'...
that I was created from his rib.
But, the timing was never right,
circumstances just didn't give.
Always vowed to remain friends,
cause his spirit was truly moving.
Even through my next relationship,
which was long and unfulfilling...
Got married to the next;
but, something was wrong from the start.
I had never been so lifeless
in trying to constantly please someone.
If he didn't want to go, I didn't.
If he didn't want to do, I wouldn't.
Went from being a sex-o-holic
to "I could care less if I did it."

Not going to harp too long over this tried,
but truly failed attempt...
to be happy with the one I vowed
to spend the rest of my life with.
It didn't work, cause he lost sight
of what was standing right beside him.
Didn't appreciate who I was...
never tried to make amends.
Cried my last cry and got divorced
after ten long years.
Moved on with my life...
no more thoughts, no more tears.
A few months later, met someone new;
no one else compared to him.
Traveled daily from another state,
just to spend his time with me.
Sex was rather frequent...
any position, from dusk to dawn.
I still recall that Saturday
we actually ran a marathon.
His grips were something serious;
could get aroused from just the thought.
A beautiful smile, yes, he had...
was never afraid to sit and talk.
Marriage was on the tongue...
silver and black were the colors.
With a Marine by my side,
thought I had everything I wanted.

Affectionate with street smarts...
this guy was a true corporate thug.
Carried AKs and Tech 9's
for those 'just in case' moments.
Truly thought he would be the one,
but little signs began appearing.
Started hearing my spirit's voice...
but, unlike before, I didn't ignore it.
He was nice, moved me greatly,
but something just didn't feel quite right.
I thank God for my instincts...
and, to that one I said goodnight.
Found my attraction to always fall
towards light skinned, good hair men.
But, I have yet to meet that one
my grandmom showed me in my dreams.
Always tried my best to be different...
to stand out from all the rest.
Never cared about their finances...
all I wanted was their best.
No such luck in finding him, though...
cause not one would come correct.
Stayed in prayer frequently,
cause I knew what my heart lacked.
My next mate was a gentleman
who moved the depths of my mind.
Poetic and completely charming...
he found me on-line.

Beautiful was his spirit...
it inspired me to reach for the stars.
Had me writing and thinking thoughts
I never thought I would or could.
Wasn't that great of a looker,
but my mind dismissed all of that.
Cause I just knew I had finally found
what could be the love of my life.
I had never met anyone who could touch me
in the way that he did.
The way his fingertips gripped my spine,
or his lips kissed my neck.
Eating habits were not the same, though;
he liked veggies, I liked meat.
But I loved his spirituality...
he was deeply grounded, just like me.
It didn't take long for the voices
to begin singing that familiar song...
Perhaps I was growing bored,
or maybe it was a shield from up above.
All I know is that I said, good-bye...
as I always managed to do.
Had me starting to think
was it really them, or could it be me, too?
I know I have an insatiable spirit
with no problems moving on.
But, this time I really tried,
and, yet, something still went quickly wrong.

Said I was going to quit...
said the game just wasn't for me.
Until I met the next young man,
whom I thought was from my dreams.
Tall, red, pretty hair...
had his own and needed nothing.
Only wanted to be with me,
and 'that' he was constantly showing.
Love making was off the chain...
the first to repeatedly make it rain.
Had me excited and actually wanting
to do the romance thing again.
We went on dates...he made me smile...
his embrace was even nice.
With marriage and a child on the tongue,
I thought everything was right.
Never lied to him, was always upfront...
my honesty was truly our glue.
He loved me in spite of my imperfections
and wanted to see me through.
But, as always, my spirit sensed things
that were displeasing to its sight.
Began hearing and seeing things
that I couldn't dare just let slide.
Spiritually – he was lacking...
traditional ways he was set in.
Never met anyone who could
unknowingly vex my entire spirit.

But, he did, and we would clash...
to the point of me letting go.
Cause I refused to entertain a relationship
being unhappy from the start.
He apologized, and insisted that from my dreams,
he was that 'one'...
But, I couldn't fall in love with this man,
who - for me - would give his all.
Kept seeking movement of my mind
and desiring movement of my spirit.
At times I just wanted to settle;
but, my heart would not give in.
My constant prayer is always,
"Lord, keep'em moving' if they ain't right."
No desire for the wannabe's;
I only want the love of my life.
This rib placed within my side,
I know, had to come from someone.
So, I'm waiting patiently
for the Lord to finally reveal him.

**By night on my bed I sought
him whom my soul loveth:
I sought him, but I found him not.**

Solomon 3:1 (KJV)

He loves me.

He loves me not.

I love him.

I love him not.

What exactly is love?

To some, love is just a feeling, as in what you think about someone. Some say it's an action, as in the things you might do for and/or how you might treat someone. Others say it is an emotion, as in how you would relate to someone. But, no matter how one defines it, everyone is in need of it...and everyone has different ways of showing it.

So many people, including myself, have found themselves either searching for love...hoping to find love...missing love...waiting on love...praying for love...or just trying to love. But, many times these efforts are wasted because those persons either didn't know how to recognize love, or didn't know how to give and/or receive love.

If I buy her flowers and nice gifts, she'll know I love her. If I give in and have sex with him, he'll know I love him. If I give her a job with good pay, I can get her to love me. If he takes me to meet his mom, that means he loves me *and* wants to marry me. If I forgive her for cheating on me, she'll love me enough not to do it again. If he's promising to leave his wife, I can trust that his love for me is real and that we'll soon be together. If I get pregnant and have his child, he'll always love *and* never leave me.

Really? Wow! And, to think that some people actually believe those things. The sad part about all of the above is that not one of those statements has anything to do with proving and/or showing love.

Now, I am not – by any means – an expert on what love is; but, I do profess to know what love isn't. Having heard lie after lie, story after story...having witnessed deceit after deceit, affair after affair...having been told case after case, situation after situation...having seen consequence after consequence, effect after effect...I can attest and almost guarantee to know when someone *doesn't* love someone.

From crushes to puppy loves...lust to infatuations...love to being in love... courtship to marriage...it is always best to find out where you really stand with someone; and, it is especially important for you to check your *own* feelings before saying and/or giving way to the "L" word.

Having often gotten caught up when the word, love, was used, I can truly say that I've had my own share of deceptions. I've also had my own share of realizations.

From about the age of 12, I've always dreamed of having my very own prince charming come to whisk me away...to love and to cherish me for the rest of my life. Since my early twenties, I've been hoping that my knight in shining armor would appear, make his move, capture my heart, and love me until the end of time. And, even through my late thirties, I was waiting for that 'one' that God was still preparing.

I used to have a pretty long list of 'requirements'...until, I began realizing that no one that I was meeting ever reached the bar. So, the thought process went from the long list to "it doesn't matter if he's a prince charming or a knight in shining armor...he just has to be a man, with morals, standards, and the characteristics of what God says a husband should be. "

All my dating life, I've had to deal with lying, deceiving, game-playing, immature, lustful, distrusting, unbelieving, egotistical, inexperienced and/or clueless men...who all claimed to have loved me...but none who could edify and sustain me. There used to be a time when I would settle for the first jock that spoke and showed some type of lustful interest in me...knowing good and well all he wanted was sex. Then, I grew to settle for anyone who sounded like he was going to do right by me...knowing good and well his intentions were false. Afterwards, I grew to settle for those who could move me in this way or that way...knowing all the time that he was lacking movement in the ways I needed most.

Time after time, I've given chance after chance...hoping that one would straighten up, hoping that one would get it right, hoping that one would prove to be that 'one.' There was disappointment after disappointment...and lie after lie...so much to the point that some have said I've managed to build a stone wall. A stone wall that's so tall and so thick that only the strongest and the most stellar could manage to crack and/or tear it down.

Wonder how it all got started...

Take One: My first crush.

I was 12; he was 13...cute, charming, and well-liked by all of the neighborhood girls. Did I even have a chance, being the tomboy that I was? Probably not...but, I tried anyway...only to quickly find out I could never be the *only* one. But, it didn't matter to me at that time. You see, I thought I was in love with him...and, whatever time I could get from him, I was satisfied. Even after he messed around repeatedly on me with my play cousin...even after the blood test said he wasn't the father... even after he got married to a girl I felt was not right for him...even after I ended up getting married to someone else, I still felt mad love for him... and often found myself wondering, 'what if...'

We always kept in touch, simply because his mom was really close with my family...but, it wasn't until after we both got divorced and had a few post-divorce conversations...it wasn't until after I had forgiven him for all of the hurt that he brought upon me...it wasn't until after I finally got to feel what it feels like to make passionate love with him...it wasn't until after all of that that I realized just how deep my feelings for him really were. I was merely...infatuated. I liked what I saw...the cuteness...the popularity...the charm. But, love...was never a factor. He couldn't love me before or then, because his heart was always with another. And, I could never love him, because I refused to be second.

Take Two: Puppy love...with a grown man.

I was 13; he was 20...muscular, masculine, experienced, charming...and appeared to be so genuinely into me. With just three words, he had me; and, it didn't take long for him to convince me to let him show me just how much. I lost my virginity to this man, got in trouble for this man, took risk after risk with this man, gave chance after chance to this man...only to find out that I wasn't in love with this man. Mostly because I finally realized he didn't really love me...he was just having a lustful relationship with an inexperienced girl...and, come to find out, I wasn't the only one.

I thought I could sway him...but, his player card had not expired. I thought I could change him...but, his ways were already set in stone. I thought after having his child, he would be there...but, after two years, I found out that all he wanted was to continue having relations with *me*. The child we made was of no importance to him...and, with that being said, how could I *truly* be? That was the extent of my puppy love. It ended there...right then and there.

Take Three: The boyfriend.

Tall, charming, funny, a bad boy with a good side. Met him through a phone conversation between some high school friends...and the love sparked from there. I liked him. My first real date was with him. My first orgasm was with him. I learned to shoot my first gun with him. I felt secure when I was with him. I felt loved by him, and I loved him. But, because we lived so far from each other, and our paths were quickly heading in opposite directions, we began to grow apart...and, it was only a short time after that that I began realizing that my reality was actually a fantasy.

I thought he was my prince charming...but, he wasn't there to stay a lifetime. I used to always say that the stars were not aligned for us. Or, that perhaps the timing just wasn't right. Whatever the case was, this so-called puppy love never grew into a full-grown love. And, although I still – to this day – sometimes wonder what he's doing, who he's with, if he's married, yet...I quickly remind myself that it wouldn't even matter. I loved him; but, I wasn't in love.

Take Four: The nice guy.

Funny and able to make me laugh. Kind with gentle ways. I liked him...but, wasn't moved by him. His family was nice. He drove a nice car. We went to the same community college together. But, for some reason, I wasn't able to get into him like I was with my last.

Having moved away from home during the time I was with him, I began to grow distant. Mostly because I was beginning to experience freedom on a whole different level. New guys. Different guys. More interesting guys. More experienced guys. The point is...guys. I became distracted...and foolish. I began taking this one for granted...even began lying to him...acting as if I was pregnant and needing to get an abortion, just to get some money. I knew it was wrong. I was wrong. The last time I saw him, I wanted so badly to tell him the truth...to apologize for deceiving him...but, the words never came out.

I never loved him; but, I truly did like him. He was a nice guy who only tried to do the right things...and, I took advantage of him. The first one...the last one...the only one...that *I* truly owe an apology to.

Take Five: My bestest friend.

An artist, who also knew the art of love-making. This encounter, although nice, was – no doubt – one of my unhealthiest. I was flirting around with a guy who was separated from a mentally unstable wife. Can you say, 'drama to the third degree?' I really enjoyed our conversations, the temptations and our relations... but, the abuse and frequent arguments from his wife was too much for me to watch. I found myself wanting to provoke situations, just because I felt the need to upset her. I even found myself coming close to popping a few caps in and/or around her. It was then that I began realizing that I didn't want to deal with and/or associate myself with this type (or any other type) of drama. So, I let go; but, vowed to always remain friends.

Life went on...I got married...he later got divorced. But, through it all, he was always there to offer a listening ear and an encouraging word. When I was at my lowest in my marriage, he was there to lift my spirits, to give me friendly and spiritual advice, to try to keep me on the right track – all without trying to coerce me into committing adultery, etc...which all said, to me, that he truly loved and cared for me. I think it's just a shame how, after I got divorced, my love for him wasn't as strong as it once was. I realized this after he kind-of proposed to me. To this, I claim bad timing...because I truly feel that out of all of my ex's, he would have been the one more prone to being my soul mate...my life long mate. But, my spirit said, 'no,' and I had to listen.

Take Six: The "I do...I don't" one.

Cute, but arrogant. Smooth talking, but not sincere. Settled, but still looking. This relationship was strained from the very beginning...betrayal, lies, deceit, selfishness...should I go on? I gave chance after chance, had talk after talk, made attempt after attempt...and still, nothing lasted. This made it hard to love him, let alone be *in love* with him. I didn't feel it before we married. I didn't feel it on our wedding day. I didn't feel it after having his child. I didn't even feel it after being married for the many years that we were. I cared for him and loved him, but never felt that kind of love that a wife should feel for her husband...mostly because I didn't respect him. I didn't adore or admire him. I didn't believe in him. I didn't trust him. Heck, I didn't even like him.

But, I gave my all to this relationship...I did things for him...to him...with him...because of him...to please him...to keep him...to show him...that I wanted things to work. But, what did I get in return? I got low self-esteem...a child he didn't [initially] want...years of emotional anguish... and a weakened and highly wounded spirit. But, in the end, I couldn't blame him. I had to blame myself, instead...because I knew, from day one, what I was dealing with...what I was getting myself into. All the time thinking that he would change...all the time thinking things would get better...but, he didn't and they never did. And, that, my friend, was our downfall.

Take Seven: The corporate thug.

I had just started trying the internet-dating thing...and, to my surprise, got swooped up by a very charming, and mentally stimulating man. He knew just what to say...and how to say it. We met, after only a week of conversing, and I was immediately drawn to him. He was tall, neatly groomed and had a smile that could melt the hearts of the hardest female villains around. I was taken by this guy. His charm, spontaneity, sex-drive and determination to prove his love for me were all great traits...even had me thinking of marriage again. But, something just wasn't right.

Perhaps it was his need to carry AK's and Tech 9's...perhaps it was because none of his baby mamas were cordial with him...perhaps it was because he always displayed distrust and anger towards certain types of people...perhaps it was because he was a devil-dog (Marine). Whatever, it was, my spirit constantly screaming "NO" had me more than a little worried. Was he living a side life that I didn't know about? What about him had I not learned, yet? I never was told anything, other than the fact that he just loved guns...but, it wasn't enough to satisfy and/or calm that voice in my head. I refused to get involved with another man when everything in me was saying, 'Let him go.' So, I listened...and I let him go.

Take Eight: Spoken word at its greatest.

Met this guy on-line, as well...and will admit that out of all of my previous loves, this one is the only one to succeed in totally capturing, nurturing and stimulating my mind. I felt love for this man, before I had even laid eyes on this man... which, in a sense was a good thing, because had I saw him first, I would not have even taken the time to get to know him...nor, would I have learned or experienced what a truly humbled spirit was like. He wasn't my ideal type – appearance-wise; but, he was calm...always. Gentle...always. Compassionate...always. I called this man, beautiful...not because of his looks, but, because of the spirit that he possessed. I actually had thoughts of us going somewhere...even though he was a Vegan and I was a meat lover...even though he was shy and reserved and I was outgoing and outspoken...even though he didn't have near the experience I had or I felt he needed to have, and I had been there and done that...even though he rarely had time to spend and I was always making time.

But, then...I realized...I didn't love this man. I loved what his words said to me...I loved how his fingertips on my spine made me feel...I loved how his kisses upon my neck left me with warm and fuzzies. But, none of these were enough to satisfy me...and eventually, I started hearing that familiar voice again...that "No...let him go" voice. So...I had to do it, again. I let go.

Take Nine: The drama seeker.

As a matter of fact, I don't even know why I'm including this one in my "Relationship" lineup. It probably qualifies as a fling...a fling that went from good to worse. But, because I actually gave him a chance, I've decided to include him anyway.

He was a fairly nice guy from a small, country Georgia town. Met him through a mutual friend who thought he would be a good catch. He called. We talked...went out. Was told he had been celibate for three years, and that he wanted to take things slow. Slow? Wow...that's a change. But, I needed that change. I wanted that change. I needed someone to finally get to know me...before wanting to "get to know me." But, it didn't quite happen like that. One night after a long day at work, I gave him a nice, long back massage, sealing it off with a kiss upon his shoulder blade...and, wham...that celibacy thing was shot down with the quickness. After two days, he said I was 'the one'. The next day I was given a key to his home...and was told to come over anytime. But, something must have alerted that inner me...cause quickly that voice came-a-running...again.

I recall him telling me how he never went searching for whether or not someone was cheating on him, etc...because God always managed to place the evidence right into his hands. And, amazingly, I quickly found his statement to be true. I was trusting in him, and God placed his game right into my hands. Found out he had another chick in another state. Found out he was a liar, a very bad liar. Found out he was an inexperienced player who had not even learned how to play. Found out he was a fan of drama, mistakenly thinking that I was going to play a part in providing him with continued entertainment. But, I'm not the one. I wasn't the one.

And, before he got killed, and she got mucked up, I thought I'd listen to that voice [again] and let it all go. He wanted to remain friends...but, I didn't need a friend like him, nor did he deserve a friend like me.

Take Ten: Close...but not close enough.

Tall...handsome...good. I had never met anyone who gave his all to prove his love for me...who would try repeatedly – over and over again – to get me to love him...back. In the beginning, I thought he was 'the one'...met him on-line, and was moved by his approach. Our first date was awesome...a picnic at the drive-in.

Cute...different...nice. And, his ability to make it rain...repeatedly... was even nicer. My family loved him...all seemed to think he was 'the one', too...but, he had little signs – here and there – that quickly made that ol' so familiar voice sound off again. He was great when he was quiet...but, when he opened his mouth, I began hearing that he wasn't where I needed him to be. Spiritually, he wasn't ready... mentally, he was too traditional... emotionally, he wasn't strong enough.

Loving this one actually hurt, because I had finally found someone who I truly felt 'loved' me – unconditionally...and, I couldn't return the favor. Despite his wishes, I couldn't force myself to fall in love with him...I couldn't force myself to pretend to love him...I couldn't force myself to settle for someone with whom my heart just wouldn't open up to...I couldn't force myself to go against that voice...that voice that has yet to steer me wrong. So, to this one, I, too, said goodbye.

Ten relationships, and a handful of flings...all gone down the drain. But, having them all led me to learning more and more about the things I wanted from a man, the things I didn't want from a man, and the things I refused to accept and/or deal with in future relationships.

My constant prayer has always been that God keeps'em moving if they're not 'the one'...and, after hearing that same, familiar voice over and over again, it has been confirmed that that voice was indeed my spirit...the spirit that God placed within me...to talk to me...to warn me...to aid in my request...of keeping'em moving.

Who Is He?

Haven't even heard his voice,
and I love the way he sounds...
Never seen one expression,
yet, I'm attracted to his smile...
Haven't even smelled his scent,
and I'm drawn to his flavor...
Not once have I felt his embrace,
but, his touch I'm constantly craving...
"Who is this man?" I ask, every night
before I lay for sleep...
hoping that he would hear me
and surprisingly appear in my dreams.
There is something to be said
about the way I think of him...
But, there's something to be written
about the way I feel for him.
He is the true definition of a man...
the ink in my pen...
the pillow on which I sleep...
the light in which I see.
Like lotion upon my skin,
or the feeling of silk from my sheets...
my body loves to feel him...
his kisses...and fingertips.
He is like jelly on my toast,
strawberries on my cheesecake...
a cold glass of lemonade
quenching my thirst on a summer day.
He is the steam from my shower...
hot, yet so relaxing...

a full body massage...
sending sweet and lasting sensations.
The rush from a parachute jump,
the flirt that makes my heart throb...
a rollercoaster I love to ride,
a constant and desired high.
A red rose that brings a smile,
a loving thought that stays on my mind...
a summer trip with only him...
a soft whisper in my ear...
The man from my dreams...
that God blew sweet life into...
packaged and delivered right to me...
and instantly I knew.
He is the true definition of a man...
in my jungle he is king...
my heart and hand belongs to one...
and his name is...

still a mystery.

**Delight thyself also in the Lord; and he
shall give thee the desires of thine heart.
Commit thy way unto the Lord;
trust also in him; and he shall bring it to pass.**

Psalms 37:4-5 (KJV)

Recoil...

Forty years, 11 relationships, numerous flings, a marriage and a divorce later...and – still – I had yet to find out what falling or being in love with someone feels like. Some said I was looking for Mr. Perfect (which only Jesus qualifies for); I said I had standards. Some said I should have just accepted and learned to love the man who's showing me love; I said I wasn't settling. Some said I was too strong-willed and strong-minded; I said I didn't have to accept nor tolerate non-sense. Some said I wouldn't let my guard down long enough to allow myself to be in love with anyone; I said no one had proven worthy. Some said I was going to be alone for the rest of my life; I said, nah, that wasn't in God's plan.

One would think, nonetheless, that out of all my relationships, I would have had at least one that led me to feeling and/or having that unconditional, I-can't-live-without-and-would-rather-die-than-be-without love; but, not one had – until my current husband, with which I will save those details for my next book. This chapter is being written to focus primarily on the ones that had me, "keepin' it moving."

Sooooo...back to the story...

I won't sit and say that all of my relationships were bad...they just weren't all that good.

Occasionally the timing would be perfect...but, most of the time the timing was not. Sometimes I had to learn some things...but, more often, I had to teach some things. Sometimes my partner and I would be in agreement...other times we would clash at the slightest of thoughts. Sometimes they truly loved me...but, most of the time, I only *liked* them. Never were any of us ever on the same page...at the same time...reading the same line...from the same paragraph.

I used to have this long list of requirements that went something like...'must be at least six-feet tall, 200 pounds, light-skinned, good haired, and bow-legged. Must have a post-high school education, a steady job with good pay, his own place, his own car…can have kids, but no baby mama drama…must be charming with a nice swag, understanding of women and experienced with relationships…able and ready to commit…must be genuine, straight-up and honest, not afraid to communicate, able to make me laugh, and always willing to listen…must be attentive, affectionate, protective, thoughtful, faithful, spontaneous, non-smoking and willing to sacrifice for the ones he loves. But, most of all, he must be God-fearing and God-loving, having complete trust, faith and hope in the power, grace and mercy of the Sovereign One.'

Now, when I look at that list, I don't see it being too much to ask for. As a matter of fact, all of those things (with the exception of the physical characteristics) should be prerequisites for *anyone* committing to a relationship. But, as I have often found out, they are the last things that most are striving to be and/or do. And, for those who claim to be, they end up actually only being about 60% of the way there…leaving the other 40% to be crap that I've found myself not wanting to deal with.

Lyfe Jennings once sang a song called, "When Will I Ever Fall In Love?" When I heard that song, I almost fell to my knees and cried, cause up until I turned forty, I was left thinking that I was the only one on earth who had yet to experience the feeling of being in love with someone. I used to always ask, what am I doing wrong? Why do I seem to keep attracting and picking guys who mean me no good? Why do I keep settling for the ones who only have about 60% of what I need to be happy…while, at the same time, tolerating the nonsense in hopes to at least get 40% more in the months to come? Why? Why? Why?

I would hear story after story about women who were happy with their mates, who were in love with their mates, who, although there were issues in their relationships, couldn't live without their mates. But, those stories were few and far between and from mostly older couples who had already been together for 15 plus years. Every other relationship

I've heard of, personally witnessed or was going through myself, was always in trouble.

It wasn't until after I had gotten saved that I began really looking at my own relationships. The main culprit of my breakups – differences. Unequally yoked differences. Another factor – insecurities. Insecurities that promoted jealousy and a diminishing trust level. And, finally...the last culprit – lust. That objectifying with no desire to really know *me* type of lust.

I'm almost ashamed to admit it; but, all of my relationships were built upon a foundation of lust and sex. Not one could I honestly say I waited past a second date to have sex with. And, most of the time, it wasn't because I wanted or had to have it; but, mostly because I was trying to please and keep the attention of the man...that, technically, but unknowingly, I had already won over [with my mind] anyway.

You see, I have learned [from watching, being around and dealing with all types of men] how to be the woman they need me to be. How to say the things they want and need to hear. How to do the things they need done. Some have actually said that I was a pimpstress, because I had a way of saying or doing things that would lure men right into my hands... that would have them almost begging to be around and/or spend time with me. I don't see me being that way at all. In fact, my stance on the matter is that I'm just a very attentive woman who always makes a point to listen. Carefully.

Being attractive was to my advantage, as well...but, I contribute my success with capturing the attention of men to be a result of the way I grew up (I am a product of my upbringing). While most girls my age grew up hanging with their girlfriends or constantly spending time in their mirrors, etc., I was always hanging around their male counterparts. Paying close attention to their mannerisms...how they would act when around someone they liked versus those they didn't like; how they would act if they were interested in a woman versus how they acted when they were not; how good they treated a woman they loved versus how they tended to dog a woman out that they didn't; the lies they would tell when they were trying to be a player, or the truth they would eventually end up telling when they got caught. Whether they were around women who made them happy, or women who seemed to strip every bit of joy they could have possibly had away...I was paying attention...to it all.

And, that, my friend, was and remains to be my advantage. My disadvantage, unfortunately, is my unfailing desire to give chances to the ones I see potential in...only to eventually find out they didn't see enough in themselves to fulfill it.

Having learned how to speak and how not to speak to a man...having learned how to treat and how not to treat a man...having learned how to flirt with, when to flirt with, and with whom to flirt with...I have in some ways mastered the skill set needed to effectively communicate with those that I like. In addition to being *naturally* kind, thoughtful, generous and caring, I was always sacrificing my needs for theirs...even when they didn't deserve the treatment I was giving.

During the last relationship mentioned in this chapter, I noticed that God was beginning to minister to me, transforming me into the woman He would have me be. I found that I could no longer lie about my feelings, nor could I continue to hold in what was bothering me. The guy I was with heard everything – whether it hurt him or his feelings or not. Now, I wouldn't intentionally say things in ways to hurt him, but some of the things I said (although they were true), I could tell would bother him...bother him 1) because they were never things that he wanted to hear, and 2) because it meant that I wasn't seeing him in the light that he so desperately wanted to portray.

But, I was growing. Mentally. Emotionally. Spiritually.

As I've mentioned before, my constant prayer has always been to "keep'em moving, if they ain't *The One*." And, then, it was to protect, cover, mold and guide that *One* that He was preparing for me. But, one day, after asking God just why it is I keep ending up with guys who just never seem to measure up, who just never seem to get it right...I received a response saying, "I am preparing *you*, as well." It was then that my eyes were finally opened. I had to go through those things, and deal with those individuals, and endure the hardships for that purpose...because God was preparing me, too...preparing me...for *my* One.

You see, as I thought about it more, I began realizing that I needed work, too. I still had buried hurts that I never let out. I was always thinking that I was okay, because I never let it interfere with my relationships. But, what I didn't realize is that my burying of those hurts didn't really release those hurts. I still carried them, and subconsciously, I still felt them.

And, after having gone through and/or witnessed all of the negative characteristics in the men I was involved with and/or hung around, I managed to build a wall...a wall full of mental bricks...bricks of notes...notes of things that I liked in a mate, notes of things that I didn't like, and notes of things that I wanted no involvement with. And, because of this, I found myself hurting so many men – unintentionally, of course – because as soon as they managed to pull one of those notes off the shelf, placing it at the forefront of my thoughts, I found that I was very quick to let go. I let go...mostly due to my spirit whispering, and sometimes screaming, those ol' so familiar no's...but, also due to my inability to stick with someone I didn't feel I could be satisfied and/or happy with.

You see, although my list of requirements had shortened somewhat, two characteristics I needed and always found myself looking for were strength and integrity. I also looked for an even temperament...mostly because temper tantrums and whining are not things I can or want to deal with. I've never tolerated it from my sons...and I definitely couldn't tolerate it coming from a man who is supposed to be my covering... which leads me to the most important characteristic of all – a man's spiritual growth.

If God has yet to pierce a man's heart, leading him into submission to God's Word and God's ways, that – to me – says he will not understand and/or know what being my covering entails...nor, will he have the wisdom and substance needed to fulfill the role as my covering. This need is critical to the success of any of my relationships; because, in order to understand me and where I am in my growth and relationship with God, he, too, would have to be focused and grounded – spiritually.

But, unfortunately, the list doesn't stop there. Just like there are strengths that I look for, I also look for a man's weaknesses...because it's the finding of those weaknesses that will help me to see if they're a keeper or let-goer. Two weaknesses that I despise, and despise greatly, are lies and drama.

Now, don't get me wrong...I tend to give everyone their fair shake of trust; but, the moment they tell that first lie is the moment that trust wall starts falling. And, drama...well, I'm not very giving to that at all. I hate being in the midst of and/or around things that cause me strife...things that vex my spirit...things that would have me questioning my value and/or risking my spirituality. On so many occasions, I chose to deal with situations which I thought were minor in relation, but actually ended up being more than I expected...more than I wanted to deal with...more than I even cared to remember.

You see, in the midst of my spiritual growth, I began realizing how much I had actually relied on men to validate me. Instead of taking the time to get to know myself, I allowed them to tell or show me who I was, based upon the issues that I always found myself dealing with. I would endure the hardship, the lies, the deceit, the preconceptions and misconceptions...everything that I knew deep within me was wrong...in attempts to prove to them that I was a *good* woman. Over and over again...until...I finally came to my senses. Or, better yet, until God finally opened my eyes.

He showed me that I didn't have to deal with, put up with or entertain the foolishness that men would try to bring into my life. He showed me that those actions being presented were not signs of love, but, instead, signs of disrespect and dishonor. That the drama I was accepting didn't prove my worth; but, on the contrary, showed how foolish I was to even think that it did.

You see, there will always be people in or around your life who mean you no good...who tend to look like real gold, but are really tarnished brass...who are so selfish in nature that they don't care enough about your feelings and/or how their actions are affecting you...but, yet are quick to proclaim how real their love is for you. It's amazing how often this happens...but, it's even more amazing how often we believe it.

Not all relationships are meant to last. Not all partnerships are going to last. In fact, some are temporary by design. God's design...for God's purpose.

Everyone who we meet and/or come into contact with is purposed. They are placed in our lives during a particular point in time to complete a mission that our Most High has set for us. He knows what you can handle and what you can't handle. He knows what you're going to do, before you even do it. Your road map was written before you were born...just as your end is already written, too. So, it is only wise to know and believe that the people you're allowed to deal with are there...for a reason.

Perhaps it is a quick encounter...one that allows someone to [in a moment's time] bring joy into your life, or you, joy into theirs. It may be through a smile or a simple compliment...a helpful hand or an unforeseen blessing...a statement made or a Word given. Another reason for quick encounters could also be to test you and your level of growth...which will serve its purpose of either showing you that you are where you should/need to be or that you have much more growing to do. Whatever it is, the encounter will be quick...and you - more than likely - will never see that person again.

Then, there are those encounters that are meant to last a little longer...for a season. In this season, friendships can be formed, trust can be gained, and relationships can be built. These types of encounters, however, generally bring along lessons...life lessons. Whether it's to teach us what we do or don't want, can or can't deal with, how or how not to handle certain situations or types of people...we are allowed to experience these encounters just long enough for us to obtain the lesson involved...and, shortly after, that person is gone.

And, finally, there are life-long encounters...meant to extend past one or all four seasons. These encounters are like marriages...that are worked on; children... that are raised; employees...that are made into managers. Not every road will be smooth; but, by the time you reach the end, you will be able to recognize and appreciate each bump (encounter) for what it was.

No matter which encounter you come into contact with, each one is designed to help you weather the storms...to teach you to appreciate the rain...to show you how to enjoy the warmth...and to get you to a point that you are able to embrace and accept the additional changes that will soon come about.

You will also find that not all encounters are pleasant ones. Like family members and so-called friends, some encounters can get up under your skin, bother you, frustrate you, deceive you, hurt you; but, you have to realize that they are there...to ultimately MAKE you.

These encounters I've referenced are and/or could be your relationships. They are definitely representations of mine. Some were short, some were long, some were so quick that I didn't get to enjoy the blink...but, I'm thankful, for each and every one, nonetheless.

All of my relationships taught me something...something about myself... something about others. All of my flings, one-night-stands, and other types of encounters helped shape me into being the woman that I am today. Each played a part in helping me to realize, rationalize, and accept them for what they were. Lessons.

In addition to learning about the things we like and/or don't like, we should let these lessons teach us about the opposite sex...how to handle the opposite sex...how to love the opposite sex. There are so many of us who grew up in single parent households that didn't quite foster to or provide a solid foundation in which we could build relationships upon; but, that doesn't mean we *can't* treat our partners with respect...that doesn't mean we *can't* be faithful and committed to our partners...that doesn't mean we *can't* trust and edify our partners...that doesn't mean we *can't* whole-heartedly love our partners. It just means we have to try harder...to endure longer...to sacrifice more.

Relationships, just like marriage, take work. The more work you put in, the better off your relationship will be. And, yeah, it takes two...but, if one starts off right, it just may very well spark the other to get right.

Once you begin to realize that the earth doesn't revolve around you...once you begin to take the focus off of the negatives that your partner inhibits...once you begin to look at the brighter side of things, you will begin to see the light that will not only enable you to stabilize your relationship, but also to prepare you for that next level – marriage. It might even be best if you went to a marriage counselor (before even the thought of marriage), to hear of and/or be mentored on things relating to you personally. We all could use a reality check every now and then.

And, if that doesn't sound appeasing, hang around some *happy* married couples in your family; or, at least get you some married friends – just so you can begin to see/hear tactics that others use to keep their relationships strong. Besides, if you never witness how a man is *supposed* to treat, protect and love a woman...if you never witness how a woman is *supposed* to submit to, support and love a man...how else would you know?

But, I don't want to throw caution to the wind...not everybody needs to be paid attention to...not every relationship/marriage is a healthy one. Hence the reason why I said hang around 'happy' married couples. Happy married couples will exhibit more positivity...more of what you need to know to keep a partnership thriving. But, be careful not to linger too long...and be careful (if you are attractive) to get most of your advice/learning from the same sex married partner. Otherwise, you may very well run the risk of having to deal with wandering eyes from their partners and/or jealous/suspicious behaviors from them. Trust me...it happens...more often than you think...from people you would never suspect... even when it's not warranted...even when you're not aware. Everything that shines is not real gold. So, be careful.

Another method to improving yourself and/or your relationships is to read up on it. Maybe. But, perhaps, a better method is to *acknowledge* [the things that you did wrong in previous relationships], to *change* [to doing the opposite in your present or future relationships], and to be *consistent* [in applying those changes]; this, by far, will be the best way for you to retain and/or grasp how best to relate to your partners.

You have to learn how to trust and how to be trustworthy. You have to learn how to listen and be listened to. You have to learn how to have faith and how to prove faithful. You have to learn how to give respect and how to earn/gain respect. You have to learn how to appreciate romance and spontaneity, as well as how to be a great lover in return. You have to learn what pain feels like, so as to not want to cause or inflict pain on someone else. You have to learn how to be forgiving, because one day, you're going to want to be forgiven.

There are so many things to learn and be mindful of while in relationships that you may feel you have to go to grad school just to get it all. But, it's really not that hard. The best and most promising way to get there is to "treat others as you wish to be treated." If you don't want to be lied to, don't lie to them. If you don't want to be cheated on, don't cheat on them. If you don't want to be unjustly accused, don't falsely accuse them. If you don't want to be smothered, don't cramp their space. If you don't like being abused or used, don't abuse or use another.

I know...you're probably saying, "that's all good and everything...but, I've been there and done that, and still I got done wrong." Well, get over that! I didn't say you wouldn't get hurt, mistreated, lied to, etc...what I am saying is that if you continue to do your part, God will make sure you get what you deserve...in due season.

No matter how much pain that person may have caused you, you *will* have victory in the end. The ones who mistreated you will – one day – after God has paid them back with not being able to find anyone as good as you, recognize and remember just how good they had it. And, the pain will then fall upon them, because they will long for you, but won't be able to have you. Or, karma will show its head and allow someone to come along and mistreat them exactly how they mistreated you. You know the old saying, 'What goes around comes around.' God doesn't like ugly, and especially if ugly is being done towards his children. So, don't worry...the evil ways of your partner or ex-partner will be handled...in due time. And, you, my friend, will be rewarded with someone so special, so loving, so caring that you can't help but to recognize, appreciate and rejoice over that *gift* that God has sent to you.

Another thing I want to note before closing this chapter is that in all that you do, get an understanding. Take time to listen to and ultimately understand your partner. Pay attention to their likes and dislikes, and do your part in making sure that they are left happy, that they are feeling secure, that they know they have the best partner in all the world. Keep them interested...meaning spice it up. Women, if you've become complacent and are no longer 'worrying' about what your hair looks like, how many pounds you've gained, how unattractive your clothing may be...snap out of that! Spice it up...or you will risk losing that man to a woman who knows just how to catch his eye. You say you don't want your man cheating on you...then, don't give him a reason. Keep in mind that men are visual creatures...what *looks* good to them *is* good...so always look your best. Don't just wear your heels to work, wear them around the house, too.

But, don't get it twisted...looks are only half the story. Every now and then, he likes for his ego to be stroked...whether it's his brain #1 or brain #2. Stroke both of them. Compliment him, show him affection, be spontaneous, know when to give him space, listen to him and love him every time like it was your first time. Trust me, the more you stroke his ego, the more he's going to keep you on his mind...which will, in turn, keep his mind off of her. Ya feel me?

And, men, if you've become so content and comfortable with your mate that you are no longer 'worrying' about the things that matter most to them, or how your six pack has turned into two spare tires, or how your once-loved swagger has fallen by the way side...snap out of that! Just like you want us to keep it hot by dressing up and role playing, etc., we want you to keep it hot, as well.

Surprise us sometimes. Cook for us sometimes. Clean the house (without being told to) sometimes. And get *off* of the couch. It's alright to have your personal time, your TV time, your time with the boys, etc...but, don't let that time consume you and/or flow into *our* time. Make time for us. Quality time. Expose us to something different. And, although sex is the bomb (for those of you who know what you're doing), know that women want to experience the joys of the *world* sometimes, too. Those four walls get pretty boring to look at – day in and day out. Ya feel me?

I promise if you can treat every day (or, at least most days) as if it was the day you first met, things would go so much smoother. Romance is necessary. Attention is mandatory. And, unexpected gestures of love, even if it's just a note on the bathroom mirror saying how much you love that person, goes a long way. It's the little things...*it's the little things*. Unless, of course, you're crazy enough to be hooked on stupid with the gold-digging-use-you-for-all-they-can type...then, my friend, you're on your own. I have no advice for you – except to RUN. "Run, Forrest, run!!!!"

Over my course of relationships and building relationships, as well as letting go of relationships, I've learned that three words (if done consistently) will, as Keith Sweat once sang, "make it last forever." Those words are: edify, support and love. Practice those things... always. Even when you don't feel like it. Keep doing them until you've perfected them. Cause trust me...without those three – with the greatest being love, they won't be happy...and neither will you.

Like academic lessons learned in school, life has its share of lessons, as well. You can either read my words and take heed to my advice, or you can skim over them as if it was material you can't use. But, when that pop quiz comes up and finds you not prepared...don't dare say I didn't tell you so.

A note to remember: It is when we endure pain that we learn to appreciate pleasure. It is when we appreciate pleasure that we learn to love life.

Never let anyone devalue you...dishonor you...disrespect you. Always know who you are, what you are, and what you are capable of being.

You are somebody...who deserves to be loved, cherished and adored...and anyone who treats you anything less is not worthy of you. God loved you...enough to create you. God created you...enough to make you. God made you...enough to show you...just how valuable you are to Him. And, unlike others, He will never hurt you, deceive you, belittle you or leave you...you can always depend on Him, trust in Him, believe in Him. He loves you...unconditionally...faithfully... and tirelessly...in spite of your imperfections and/or wrong doings. His love is not based upon your looks and/or what you can give...but, instead upon your heart and the love that you are willing to share.

These are the things that we should look for in a mate, as well. Nothing more. Nothing less. If they have a heart as pure and/or similar to God's...they are...the *one* for you. For it says, a man is to love his wife as Jesus loved the Church. And, we all know that Jesus gave his life...for the Church. The Bible also says that a woman is to submit herself to her husband, as if she was submitting to the Lord, for the husband is the head (covering) of the wife, as Christ is the head of the Church.

If you learn nothing else from this chapter, please, please, please retain the following: Life is too short to be unhappy with someone you're not equally yoked with...and it's definitely too short for you to continue making your or someone else's life miserable. So, in troubled times, make that list (the good vs the bad)...consult with God (your only true advisor)...and then wait *and* listen for His response (through His Word). And, when you finally get that response, follow His direction (His will for your life).

Cause, trust me...He will never, ever steer you wrong.

ROUND SEVEN:
ESTEEMLESS

What is self-esteem?

And, just how do you increase it?

If someone says they think you're pretty,

do they really mean it?

If they say, "great job you've done,"

how sincere would they be?

If you never said these things,

what would that do to me?

Always tried to measure up...

to be just like the in crowd.

But, while they were standing a size 2,

I was sitting a size round.

From the moment I began examining myself,

things just were not right.

From the slow growth of my hair,

to my eyelashes that curled tight.

Always said I was cursed,

cause I had so many unwanted flaws.

A big forehead, rough hands,

and the shape of my nose.

Bad skin, stretch marks,

small breasts and a flat rear.

Never was able to obtain that six pack

no matter how many sit-ups I did.

High waist, pale skin,
fingers that were genetically wrinkled.
Long legs but short torso resulted
in an unproportioned middle.
Genetics played their part...
my upper arms were bigger than most men's.
And, although my teeth were fairly straight,
the gap really bothered me.
Stood tall, but for some reason,
I've always wanted to be short.
Although it helped (in my older age)
to equally distribute the weight out.
So many things and in so many ways
I let others depict my worth.
If I wasn't thanked or appreciated,
that, too, would bring on hurt.
Was always trying to do something nice,
to gain someone else's approval.
And, when my existence was no longer valued,
I quickly kept it moving.
I can't say I was all that bad,
cause the men seemed to like me.
But, were they really liking me?
Or, just what they thought they could get?
Women my age couldn't stand me,
they always appeared to be jealous.
"Of me?" I would always ask...
wow, look at their esteems.

But, anyway, I know how they feel...
I see pretty women all the time.
And, still wish, to this day,
that I had something that they had.
To be wealthy, I've always wanted...
had to keep up with the Jones'.
Can't tell you how bad it felt
to lose my most favorite vehicle.
Dropping back down to a 10-year-old car
was unheard of for me.
That was failure coming from the woman
I had grown up to be.
Wanted so badly to be envied
for the things I had and could have.
Wanted to feel I was on top,
cause nothing else got me there.
Always strived to do my best
on every job I was ever in charge of.
Work was always loved,
but insecurities kept my mind jumbled.
Always said I could have done better,
if I had added that one extra piece.
A perfectionist I claimed to be,
but, I realized that was killing me.
Working 24 hours a day,
racking my brain over the simple stuff.
Stressing my body with unnecessary
worries when no one else even cared.

Was married to a guy whose idea
of romance was just about having sex.
Can't tell you how hurt I became
when my advances were dismissed.
No flirts, no surprises,
nothing special shown on those other days.
Really had a girl wondering,
'is there someone other than me?'
Used to always say it was he
who caused my low self-esteem.
Until a friend once broke it down
that it was called, 'self' esteem.
I had to learn to value myself
by doing whatever I needed to do.
I had to learn to love myself
before I could expect anyone else to.
Rather than being a perfect rock,
I'd claim to be a flawed diamond.
Cause with all of my imperfections,
I'm still, to me, quite worthy...
of all the love that God
can possibly give and see me handling.
I'm my own woman...
who's now proud of the skin He's blessed me with.

**For God hath not given us the spirit of fear;
but of power, and of love, and of a sound mind.**

2 Timothy 1:7 (KJV)

They say you're supposed to love yourself.

But, what if you don't like yourself?

They say you're supposed to be yourself.

But, what if you can't stand yourself?

The skin you're in...

The hair you have...

The size of your clothes...

The shape of your nose...

The heaviness in your hips...

The fullness of your lips...

What if...you don't like yourself?

All my life, I've had to deal with my hair not being long and pretty like the other girls...with my hips and breasts not maturing as quickly and/or voluptuous as the other girls...with my skin not being as silky smooth and perfectly colored as the other girls...with my teeth not being as straight and pearly white as the other girls...with my hands not being as soft or as pretty as the other girls...

So many things I felt I could complain about...and so very often, I did. And, getting older...didn't help.

One week shy of my 16th birthday, I gave birth to a son. Loved him...but, he could have kept the stretch marks. Around my hips, on my waist and surrounding my belly button. Yeah, he could have really kept those. Although, I will admit that the stretch marks around my navel kind of resembled sunrays that most thought was a tattoo. But, that bulge at the base of my abdomen that has yet to go away, is still – to this day – bothersome.

But, not as bothersome as the cellulite that managed to surface in my early thirties. What?! Dimpling in my thighs. Wow!! So, not only can I not wear short-torso or bikini bathing suits (due to my abs not being perfectly sculptured and my stomach being marked with pregnancy scars); but, I also have to resort to wearing shorts to the pool (to hide the cellulite)? Wow!! It just gets better and better.

I will stop there, however...cause I do have a couple of physical characteristics that I am proud of...like the bow in my legs and the seductiveness in my eyes. Everything else...if I could recreate and/or make anew, EVERY THING else would probably be made anew. They better be glad I haven't won the lottery...cause that choice between taking the red pill or the blue pill...I would have to say that I would have probably paid to have the best of both worlds.

Aside from my physical imperfections (that led me to esteeming myself lower than what I should have), I've also had issues with letting others depict my self worth.

I can recall times – as a child – trying to befriend females my own age...only to get picked on or looked down upon...only to get talked about or ridiculed. No, I couldn't do cartwheels or skate on rollerblades...and, no, I wasn't interested in polishing my fingernails...and, no, I wasn't even interested in the silly girl talk that they used to have...but, that didn't warrant me being excluded from their group(s).

I used to buy candy and give it away. I used to not eat lunch, just so someone else could have extras. I used to let others cut in front of me in lines, just so they didn't have to stand so long...all in attempts to one day be seen as an equal...or, at least to be liked and/or accepted.

As a teen-ager growing into my own, I still found myself trying to fit in with others my age, only to get rolled eyes, stuck up noses, and the pretention that they didn't hear me speak to them. Sometimes – I have to admit – it would hurt...it would hurt deep. So deep that I used to question myself all the time as to what could be wrong with me. I used to think I had the word 'witch' written all over my forehead that only others could see; because, other than this, them not accepting me just didn't make sense to me...and, honestly, it still doesn't.

I used to try to hang around the outer circles, which were just close enough to the real circles to make it seem like I might have been in someone's clique. I really wanted to be. Everywhere you turned, all you would see is groups of pretty girls, groups of smart girls, groups of misfit girls...you even had the groups of nerdy girls. Everybody seemed to fit somewhere...except for me. I had no group, no clique...no one to roll with.

For years...I grew up...a loner.

It was so hard trying to gain female friends my own age that I eventually decided to just ignore them...and instead, go after making male friends. After all, the boys seemed to be more accepting, more inviting, more willing to befriend me...and, even though they picked on me, too, their pickings were much more tolerable.

I had hung around boys so much that I began to do the things they did...from riding on huffy bikes with them, to jumping over fences like them, to playing street ball with them, to talking trash like them, to break-dancing in the parking lot like them, to fighting like them. And, although I was beginning to feel valued, because I finally was able to fit in somewhere, things still were not where they needed to be.

In the sixth grade, I can recall being told that I walked like a boy. I used to have the same little pimp in my stride that they had...which ultimately gave the girls another reason to talk about me. Now, I was labeled as a dike...because my walk wasn't as feminine as theirs. By the time I started high school, I was still pimping; but, it wasn't bothering me.

I had three guys who were my closest friends...who I would talk trash with in the hallways, who were proud to hang around me, who were thankful to just be able to stand beside me. They said me being pretty and easy to get along with was what attracted them to me. I was cool...down to earth...and totally able to relate to them. I didn't nag, fuss, or belittle them. I, instead, uplifted them, and made them feel like men. I liked them, and they liked me. And, everyone else...well, they could [and did] get the finger.

That all changed, however, when my mom moved. A new school. New people. And, not one did I find to be to my liking. I walked the hallways...alone. I ate in the cafeteria...alone. I did almost everything... alone.

But, after looking at myself one day in the mirror, and after continuing to hear school mates talking about my walk, I decided that it was time for me to start becoming more lady-like. To develop a new image. To try to transform my walk from a pimp to a nice feminine swag. To somehow turn heads, not for the bad, but for the good. And, by the end of my junior year...I was finally there.

I can recall a few freshmen coming up to me in the cafeteria one day asking if they could sit with me at "my table." One girl stated she admired the way I dressed, and that she wanted to be just like me when she got older. I was flattered; because, for the first time, I was genuinely 'accepted'...by a girl. But, that was the only one.

Why am I like this? Who cares what other people think of me? I have to value myself before someone else can, right? It still pained me... however...to the core.

I finally managed to befriend someone in my senior year. We were opposites in nature...I was quiet and reserved...she was a little on the wild and crazy side. But, we clicked. We had a lot of things in common – molested by boyfriends of our mothers, mistreated by our mothers, both of us had given birth to sons out of wedlock, and we were graduating in the same year. Yeah, I had finally made a female friend...but, as like everything else...she was the only one.

I spent years being alone. But, I'm not complaining. Spending all of that time alone enabled me to do a lot of people watching. Just like I used to watch men, I used to watch women as well. I found most women to be caddy, selfish, conceited, and whiney. I also found that most of them weren't worth the time of day that many of these men gave them...that many don't even know how to respect and treat themselves, let alone someone else...that many were clueless on how to talk to and deal with men, how to handle men, how to love men...that many were backstabbing, insensitive and fast hot-tails who cared about nothing but Benjamins and Drama...but, mostly, I found that I had something to be thankful for. Women like them gave little ol' me a reputation that was so unique that all who came into contact with me could recognize and appreciate...

...that fact that I wasn't like *them*.

Not Like Most

She's hungry, yet full...thirsty, yet quenched...
aroused, yet satisfied...disappointed, yet content.
Invincible to some, misunderstood by others...
approached by many...but, not one can hold her.
Insatiable she used to be,
or perhaps she still is...
cause she has yet to find that one
who gave her life through his rib.
She's tired, yet patient...lonely, yet accompanied...
weak, yet strengthened...thanks to her beliefs.
She's passionate about her doings,
a true sista by birth...
but, she refuses to let life's dramas
corrupt and change her.
Hated on constantly by those
that see but don't know her...
Her swagger is something serious;
her touch, always welcomed.
Sexy is not the word for
she gleams seduction with just the slightest.
Calm is her nature,
but she's aggressive when he isn't.
Genuinely thoughtful...
her generosity is extreme.
Her sexuality is addictive...
her aurora, captivating.
An expert with expression...she listens, and then she speaks.
Only during one prized act will her 'stops' not mean quit.
Charming with her romance...
it's flavorful like the sweetest wine...
Extremely good for the heart,

but even better for the mind.
Not many know how to handle,
not many know where to start...
One must move the depths of her mind
if they want to capture her heart.
No skeletons are in her closet...
lies she will never tell.
An angel so well disguised,
you'd first think you were going to hell.
Intelligent with street smarts,
she can keep it hot without a doubt.
Not just questions will be asked,
but your actions will be watched.
Don't take kindly to playing games,
and being used is the worst...
She can be your best friend,
or for your mind a driven hearse.
Poetry is her outlet,
an ocean's breeze is always a plus...
She's drama free for those who wonder,
so stay away if you've got mess.
A real sweet nature she does possess...
she loves to smile, loves to laugh...
enjoys the simple things in life,
and could care less about your cash.
Material things are good to have,
but are not necessary for her happiness.
She's supportive of the ambitious one,
and your back she'll always have.

She Is...Not Like Most.

**Humble yourselves in the sight of the Lord,
and he shall lift you up.**

James 4:10 (KJV)

Recoil...

Beyoncé...Sanaa Lathan...Taraji P. Henson...Nia Long...Serena Williams...Rihanna...Jada Pinkett-Smith...Nicki Minaj...Angela Bassett...Janet Jackson...Tina Turner...Tyra Banks... Alicia Keys...Mary J. Blige...Oprah Winfrey...Michelle Obama. What do they all have in common? Beauty. Black beauty. Breath-taking, natural beauty. The kind of beauty that leaves women like me wishing...wishing we had hips like them, thighs like them, arms like them, skin like them, hair like them...wishing we could walk like them, talk like them, sing like them, act like them...wishing we had their charisma, their poise, their glow.

Now, some would look at me and say that I have nothing to complain about... that I'm beautiful...that I'm poised...that my swagger is both stunning and captivating. Some would even say that my presence is refreshing and delightful, and that I would have no problems running with and against the best of them. But, it wasn't always that way...

You see, as a youngster, I felt like the red-headed step child who just couldn't measure up to any of my peers. They all had long hair; mine was short. They all wore clothing from the Gap and Rich's; I wore Sears and K-Mart. They lived in big houses; I lived in the projects. They had all the cute boys swarming around them; I had Tyrone and 'em.

As I mentioned previously, it wasn't until my junior year in high school that I began to really come out of my shell – that ugly duckling shell. In a sense, I guess I shouldn't be that hard on myself, as I truly don't think I've ever been unattractive...just never the *ideal*.

You know, like those models in the magazines. The size zeroes with super smooth skin and flawless makeup. Those were the *ideals* when I was growing up. And, then...TLC came out with that song, "Unpretty." You could buy yourself some hair [extensions] if you desired long hair. You could have plastic surgery on your nose, if you didn't like the shape of it...et cetera, et cetera.

For years, I was five-feet-eight-inches, weighing in at 135 pounds. Married, weighing in at 152 pounds. Divorced, weighing in at 170 pounds. Now, for my height, that weight was distributed nicely, although a flat stomach and toned arms would have done wonders to compliment my hips, bowed legs, and stance. But, no such luck with that.

It has taken years for me to come to grips with my appearance...to recognize and accept the fact that God made me...according to His perfect Will. And, it was my choice to alter that look by not taking care of myself in the manner in which I should have. I complained about my weight, yet, I kept snacking on unhealthy foods. I complained about my hair being short, yet, I kept cutting it every time I took my braids out. I complained about the bulge in my stomach and my flabby arms, yet, I sat on the sofa watching television, instead of pulling that elliptical out of the closet. Yeah, I am the way I am because of me and my careless behaviors.

I truly commend those women who actually put in the necessary work to transform themselves into looking better, feeling better, being better. And, although it has taken me years, I am proud to say that not only have I recognized the root causes of my low self-esteem, but that I have also began doing things to increase and maintain it.

I may still try to complain about the stretch marks and the less than fit abs, but, I really have no reason to. I've grown to realize that worrying about my extremities not measuring up to the figure eight models on television and in magazines is not going to do me any good. Heck, I don't even want to be their size...cause I know spending my days being miserable eating only broccoli and carrots, and sweating my perm out every day is not what I want to be doing, or how I want to be living.

I chose, instead, to be more health conscious...to watch and cut down on the foods that are not good for me...to eat more of the foods that are...and to become more active – through walking, dancing, and exercising in my home. I can now stand proud (even at 165 pounds) knowing that this vessel that God has created is unique and still loved, no matter how I elect to view myself. The most interesting fact that I've had to learn is that I was the *only* one who actually saw me in a negative light.

I know they say beauty is in the eye of the beholder. That – it truly is. But, unfortunately, beauty sometimes comes with a hefty price. Some people tend to think that just being a pretty woman [or a handsome man] is worth its weight in gold. But, in actuality, not all beautiful people enjoy being that way. You see...I started out this chapter telling you how ugly I felt I was...but, after being shaped and transformed into the woman that I am today, the struggles are of a rather different kind.

I'm sure you've heard that beauty on the inside counts more than beauty on the outside. This statement is true (to the intelligent mind). But, having the best of both worlds – both inner and outer beauty – can sometimes feel as if one was cursed.

From being a people watcher all my life...to having to experience both good and evil throughout my life...to being humbly molded and lovingly shaped by the Most High...to listening – attentively – and unselfishly giving of myself, I have become what some might call "too good to be true."

I've always made it a point to treat others as I wished to be treated... to show care and concern towards all that I came into contact with... to always be watchful and mindful of the words that I allowed to come out of my mouth...to always try to be on my best behavior, no matter what circumstances present themselves. I've always tried to get along with everyone...to reach out to people on their level, so as not to make them feel as if I thought I was better than them, or, on the contrary, that I was less worthy. I demanded respect, but I also gave it. I commanded attention, but I also showed plenty of it.

These things, coupled with being very easy on the eyes, have made many look at me through glorified eyes...but, there were always those who felt better when they could look at me through filthy and faulty lenses.

I've tried my best to make all feel comfortable around me, but I get blamed for doing things that I had not once thought about...that I had not one intention of doing. One of the biggest and most hurtful comments I've heard, thus far, is that I'm "good at reeling in all of the [single or taken] men, only to hurt them by leaving them, which makes for stale left-overs for the – quote – sistas who were *more deserving* of them anyway." Now, that comment alone spelled hatred... but, even more so, it spelled pain...pain to know that they thought I was to blame for capturing and taking the eyes and attention of men (and nowadays, lesbians) from them. Like I purposely and strategically enticed men to walk right past them and approach me...like I telepathically told those same men that no other girl in the room could measure up to me...like the covering of my size 36B cups actually had men imagining all of the ways and all of the things that they could do with and to me. Right!

Some say I command attention when I walk in a room...I say I just have a rather confident walk. Some say that my physical attractiveness lures men, and my having a beautiful mind and a magnetizing spirit captures them...I say glory be to God for placing His light within and around me. Some say I should sit down when there are other single women in a room, so that guys will take notice to them first...I say I've tried that in baggy sweatpants and a t-shirt, and I still got approached.

I think it all boils down to that 'light' that illuminates from within me. To have gone through all that I've gone through, and still remain loving, thoughtful, caring, and good-natured towards others says a lot...about the power of God. And, even though I don't like the attitudes received from women, and the often unwanted advances received from men, I believe that says a lot, too...about the will of God.

You see, if I hadn't thought less of myself at one point in my life, I wouldn't be able to see why I should think more of myself today. Why I should esteem myself higher...why I should be thankful for every flaw that I have. God truly has a way of keeping one humbled, and I thank Him. Cause, you see, if He allowed me to take all of the attention that I received to my head, I would be so full of myself that I wouldn't be able to see that it is He who is working in me...that it is He that is molding and shaping me...that it is He who is transforming me...that it is His light that is gleaming from within me...and not my own.

If we take a moment to look at ourselves, despite whatever flaws we think we see or have, we will come to realize and appreciate the fact that God made us that way. Some people complain about how big their nose is...not taking into account that there are some people on this earth who can't even smell. Some people complain about how big their feet are, while there are folks on this earth who don't even have the pleasure of feeling or walking on their feet...heck, some don't even have feet.

And, then, there are some people who are so negatively affected by misfortunate accidents which may have left them immobile that they fail to realize that just the fact that God spared their life means they are still useful. We take so many things for granted. We find so many things to complain about. We are so unappreciative of the gifts that God continues to bless us with on a daily basis. Heck, some of us don't even take one moment out of each day to just say "thank you, Lord" for anything.

If you're still living...you're good. If you're still breathing on your own...you're good. If you still have vision (even if it is assisted with glasses or contacts), you're good. If you still wake up in your right mind, and are able to put on your own clothes and eat food from a fork that you can hold...you're good. Cause it could all be gone...in a blink.

We should learn to be (if not already) grateful for the skin we're in...grateful for the body we're in...grateful, because what we don't know and/or are failing to realize, is that things could be 'worse.'

You could be homeless...strung out on drugs...or, even dead. And, I know... some of you are probably saying to yourselves that that would be better than being toothless, hairless or fat. And, if you're thinking that way, hold on...let me get this laugh out. Ha. Ha. Ha.

The sad part about this is that I have no pity for those who harbor those kinds of thoughts. Because, see, if you have those thoughts, it means you have yet to realize the greatness of God. It's not what's on the outside that matters (most); but, what's on the inside. Give yourself a good, long look...then, ask yourself:

"What about me do I *like*?"

"What about me is attractive to others? The opposite sex? My elders? My children? My peers? Me?"

"What can I change about myself to make me feel better about myself?"

"Do I have the will-power to do it?"

Do you know that just changing your attitude about your appearance and/or demeanor can make a world of difference for your self-esteem? Do you know that if you began loving yourself, what others think of you wouldn't even matter? Do you know that if you focused on the love that God has for you, the lack of love from others would not be a care or concern of yours?

You should truly try being grateful for the life that God has blessed you with. You should try being grateful for the body that God has blessed you with. You should try being grateful for the inner beauty that God has blessed you with. For, when you've been blessed by Him, you are indeed worthy. You are indeed beautiful.

Besides, why want to be a perfect rock, when being a flawed diamond is worth so much more?

ROUND EIGHT:
DOLLAS 2 CENTS

$4.75 was the hourly wage
received at my first part time job.
But, of course this had to go up,
in order to support me and my child.
Opportunities were presented,
and doors were often opened.
Never obtained my degree,
but the pay just kept increasing.
Credit score was through the roof,
could buy whatever I truly wanted.
Had four credit cards
with over 15 thousand dollar limits.
Bought two homes,
rode in new cars every other year.
To me, I was still lacking,
but to others, I was rich.
Though sometimes depleting my resources,
I felt good when able to help
family and friends keep
their lights on and/or their stomachs fed.
Never once had a bill
that I couldn't pay in full each month.
Holidays were done big...
everybody got the gifts that they wanted.

I can attribute some of this, though,
to me having help with the mortgage.
I was married through these times,
so, money issues were not pressing.
He had his own, and so did I...
other than the house, no joint accounts.
But, everything began to fall
around and after my divorce.
I had heard there would be consequences,
a wrath I'd have to feel.
For doing something God didn't like,
just because I was weary.
Tried my hardest to hold on
to the lifestyle I'd grown to admire.
Trying to keep up with the Jones',
instead of appreciating what I had.
Lost some things in the process,
due to careless financial tactics.
No longer was I the Bank of Bodie...
'cause no longer did I have it.'
Credit companies were harassing...
constantly breathing down my neck.
"How you think I'm gonna pay you,
 when I can barely pay my rent?"
Caller ID was something serious...
glad I had it on every phone.
I just wanted them to go away...
I just wanted to be left alone.

Consulted with some lawyers
to see just what they could do for me.
I laughed and cried at the same time,
cause to the system, I was rich.
Had a brand new SUV,
with navigation and the works.
I truly cried like a baby
when they made me give it up.
House went shortly after,
cause my ex failed to do his part.
And, it all came tumbling down
when I got garnished on my job.
Went immediately to file for bankruptcy,
cause I was drowning in this rain.
Having to rely on the help of others
I was hurt and didn't understand.
Until that day I cried my soul out
And I heard the voice of God saying...
"Asked you to try me,
but instead you wanted to hold on...
to riches that didn't belong to you...
for I was the One...
who kept all of your bills paid...
who got you those nice, new cars...
who sent your way many blessings...
who, for you, opened many doors.
All I wanted was your obedience,
to know you'd put and keep Me first.

All I wanted was your faithfulness.
I told you I'd handle the rest."
I cried, and I cried,
until the tears literally flowed no more.
Once more I heard His voice,
And everything became clear.
My faith had to be tested
And strengthened to remove the fear.
Now, I can't lie and say that times
weren't trying or were never hard.
And, I can't say that I didn't question
where the next would come from.
But, what I did do is believe
in the promises that God often gave.
And, I promise you, with God
as my witness, all has gotten paid.
Now, I'm not out of the pit, yet...
but, I can at least see a light.
I thank God for his mercy...
I thank God for his grace.

**For we brought nothing into this world,
and it is certain we can carry nothing out.**

1 Timothy 6:7 (KJV)

I live in the projects...

but, I want that mansion on the hill.

I ride on city transit...

but, I know the names of every import there is.

I can only afford second hand...

but, those new Prada's will be mine for the taking.

Mickey D's is on the menu tonight...

but, reservations I will – one day – make.

All my life I've lived a wishful life...wanting better than whatever good I saw others with...and consequently, always striving to get it.

With every promotion on my job, with every increase on my credit cards, with every bonus that came my way...you best believe I found a way to spend *every* dollar. I've never been a label chaser; but, I was always an *expensive look* chaser. Meaning...I always wanted the latest, the greatest...those things that others [around me] didn't have...those things that others [around me] couldn't get...those things that made others [around me] look up to me, as I've done [so many times] to those who had more than me. I always wanted to appear rich, because – for some reason – I thought it would make me feel rich.

You see, my first real job had me surrounded by very successful and affluent women. Sure, they were Caucasians; but, I learned a lot from every one of them...professionally and personally. I looked up to them. I admired them. I envied them. I wanted to have what they had and live like they lived.

I watched their mannerisms – how they talked, how they carried themselves, how they handled others, what they drove, the clothes they wore. Yeah, I took note of everything. And, what really touched me most was that a couple of them actually took the time to personally groom and mold me into becoming a professional and well-spoken young lady.

Don't get me wrong...my mother and other family members did their parts, too. There were many things that I admired and/or took note of from my family, as well.

My mother made a point to instill cleanliness into me. Her training is what made me the clean and well-organized person I am today. I had aunts whose homes were always show-room ready, and even those who always wore the latest fashions – and whose clothes and shoes could take up an entire living room.

I also had family members and friends who were not as fortunate in having the latest and greatest. And, after watching their lifestyles (and sometimes my own), I began to take note of things I didn't want; or, better yet, things I wanted better than. And, I'm not knocking anyone or anything...because while others may have had fine and expensive *things*, those less fortunate had fine and expensive *hearts*.

All of these things, along with God's role in not letting me have anything I didn't work [and work hard] for, played vital roles in me becoming the individual that I grew into being – a very compassionate and giving person...who just wanted to place smiles on the faces of those around me...who just wanted to live a comfortable life with no worries about where the next meal was going to come from, or how the bills were going to get paid. I continued to press my way – no matter what the cost – all in attempts to live the *good life*.

I always made a point to live in the nicest of homes, even if it was just an apartment. I always made a point to buy the nicest of cars, even if it meant me forever having a car note. I always made a point to go on weekend get-aways in super nice hotels, even if it meant me spending the last available dollar on my credit cards. I always made a point to make sure my family's lights stayed on, even if it meant me not having a spare dollar until my next paycheck.

Most of that was because I wanted to be looked upon as being a success. I wanted so badly for my sons and others to be proud of me, and my abilities. And, having things that many of my family members and friends didn't spelled accomplishment (in my eyes). I spent so much money...even money I didn't have...just to prove that I could get what I wanted...and, not so much as proof to others, but as proof to myself.

Like many of you, I'd made promises to myself when I was younger of how I was going to live better than my parents lived...of how my kids were going to have more than I had, and how they would never have to want for anything...of how my lifestyle was going to be like the rich and famous – without the celebrity drama, of course.

And, although most of those things did come true, it finally hit home as to just how deep I was burying myself. The pain of no longer being able to fulfill those promises began to surface; but, it was nothing compared to the pain of having others become witness to what felt like failure...failure that all started immediately following my divorce.

I got a higher paying job...after moving out...and, thought things were going well. But, in reality, things were getting worse.

I traded in my four-year-old car for a brand new, fully loaded SUV. I was renting an apartment that cost more than the mortgage on the house I had just moved out of. I completely furnished every room of that apartment because I refused to take any furniture from my divorce. I was even still paying my ex's utilities (in the house) up until our divorce was final...all from one income source, and some credit cards.

It seemed like the good life...for roughly five months; but, during that sixth month...all hell broke loose.

Bills were beginning to pile up, resulting in my inability to pay them in full each month. Gas prices were steadily rising, resulting in my inability to keep a full tank. My sister and brothers started spending more time at my home, resulting in additional mouths to be fed, etc. I had to stop paying tithes and offerings, cause if I didn't, my family wouldn't eat. All of my credit cards were maxed out, resulting in my inability to buy things I needed when cash was nowhere to be found. And, to top it all off, I had to accept a lower-paying job, because my current one was needing me to commit 85% of my time to out-of-state travel (which I refused to do with a young child).

No second income...no investments to cash in...no savings to pull from. I was at my wits end, with no relief in sight. I had to do something...and soon.

So, to the internet I went. I found something called, Debt Negotiation. This is where a company was supposed to negotiate with all of my credit card companies to try to get them to reduce my card balances – all for a small monthly fee. I was excited...until I realized that building the funds to pay the reduced balances on *my* credit cards would take years to get to an acceptable amount (because I owed so much on each)...until I realized that the credit card companies were not waiting to reach an agreement before hammering my credit with late payment notices (which were quickly bringing my score down from a 720 to a whopping 550)...until I realized that the constant phone calls from bill collectors were becoming more and more harassing by the day. I needed relief. And, I needed it soon.

So, I made an appointment to speak with a Bankruptcy lawyer...and almost cried in their office, upon hearing that not only would I lose my brand new SUV; but, that because I made *so much* money, I would have to pay the Bankruptcy Court one full paycheck every month for the next three years. What?!! I'm here to file for bankruptcy, because I have *no* extra money, and they – somehow – figured that I could afford to give them *half* of my monthly income??? Wow!!

I left the lawyer's office...crying...all the way home...in my car...all the way home...boo-hoo'ing...all the way home. And, when I got home, I cried some more. So much that I ended up crying out to God...

"What did I do to deserve this, Lord?" "Is this my punishment for getting divorced, Lord?" "Lord, I thought you said you would be here for me...that You would never leave me. It looks like you've left me now, Lord! What now? What now, Lord?"

I immediately became depressed. I was angry. I was hurt. "All of the things I've done for people. All of the ways I've helped people. I even kept that negro's lights on after I left him...does that not count for anything, Lord? Why me, Lord?"

After about two weeks of sulking, a friend advised me to get a second opinion; so, I did. I met with another law firm, who told me I qualified for Chapter 7 bankruptcy; and, that although I had to give my SUV back, I could always get another one shortly after my bankruptcy discharged (three months or less). Chapter 7 would mean I wouldn't have to pay back any money, which would result in me not losing a whole paycheck; and, although I was advised to find an older, less expensive car to drive until my bankruptcy discharged, I was okay with that. I left that office with a plan. I had hope. And, I was hopeful...until I went back to that lawyer's office three months later to officially file, and a new lawyer asked the question, "who told you that you qualified for Chapter 7? You only qualify for a Chapter 13, which means you have to make monthly $1,800 payments, and that you will need to remain in that 10-year old car for five more years."

I sat there...silent...tears forming in my eyes...heart sinking...anger rushing...I turned in my SUV for this 10-year old car. I had in my brain that I wouldn't have to spend money I didn't have paying back creditors...and they had the nerve to ask me 'who told me I qualified for Chapter 7?'

Five words...kept coming to the forefront of my mind: "Lord, Your Will be done." I sat there trying to convince myself that God had a plan...that this was just a test...that God didn't bring me to this point to leave me. I was literally shaking, as the lawyer kept asking me, "Do you want to go ahead and file today?"

"No. I do not."

I got up...and went home...to cry, again.

And, in the midst of those tears, I received a phone call from my ex-husband stating he was having to move out of the house (that my name was still on). "Move?" I asked..."Why?"

"I'm getting evicted...the house has been foreclosed on."

My heart sunk. Again.

What a cruel joke life was playing on me. A very cruel, cruel joke.

I got on my knees that night...and prayed like I had never prayed before...asking God to have mercy upon me...asking God to forgive me...asking God to help me...please.

Shortly after that prayer, he led me to another law firm. A law firm that stated and confirmed that I DID, indeed, qualify for Chapter 7. But, unfortunately, before my filing went through, one of my credit card companies managed to garnish one of my paychecks – 25%. Ouch. And, then, I had to pay three-hundred dollars up front and every month for the next five months (to pay for my bankruptcy). Ouch. But, okay...if it will end this madness...okay...I'm fine with that.

So, I filed. And, five months later, my bankruptcy was discharged. But, now what?

A credit score well below the noted, 'poor' level. Twenty-three percent interest on a used car loan. A credit card that I had to secure with my own money. A need to constantly rent homes, as opposed to buying them. A need to deal with lower rate companies for car insurance, etc. A need to have to pay full utility connection deposits, etc. And, then, to top it off, the inability to get a job with top employers, because they frowned upon folks who had bankruptcies or foreclosures on their records. But, the worst...having others who once looked up to you, who once thought of you as a success...others who you've often helped, often fed, and often taken care of...now be the ones that you find yourself having to call upon.

For those of you who think you're on a high and mighty cloud that you cannot and will never fall off of, take it from someone who thought the same thing. For those of you who don't believe in the statement, 'what goes around comes around', take it from someone who has lived it. For those of you don't believe in karma, take it from someone who has experienced it. It truly paid off being the generous and caring individual that I was...because during my time of need – that time that I never thought and swore I'd never see – it sure was nice having that same generosity and concern being showered back...upon me.

Broken

Broken...to have tears flowing with just the thought of it.
Broken...to feel the pain that comes when people notice it.
Broken...to be in disbelief that it could happen this way to me.
Broken...to question God as to why He was allowing it.
Broken...to try to hide from those who I felt knew me best.
Broken...to like make-up, try to cover it like a mask.
Broken...to be unable to talk when confronted by those that cared.
Broken...to look at others and scream silently, 'This isn't fair!'
Broken...to read the Bible and attend Church every Sunday.
Broken...to get an understanding as to why I was chosen.
Broken...to put that thing called pride far, far behind me.
Broken...to not only know His Word, but to put all my faith in it.
Broken...to when all else fails, fall on my knees and often pray.
Broken...to give it all up, so that a new being He could make.
Broken...to live to see blessings appear from out of nowhere.
Broken...to have my spirit touched by the love He constantly gives.
Broken...to realize that He has and must always come first.
Broken...to now I made it because – in Him – I put my trust.

And seek not ye what ye shall eat, or what ye shall drink, neither be ye of doubtful mind. For all these things do the nations of the world seek after: and your Father knoweth that ye have need of these things. But rather seek ye the kingdom of God; and all these things shall be added unto you.

Luke 12:29-31 (KJV)

Recoil...

Pain.

Pride.

Depression.

I started this chapter by telling you of how I used to live my life. But, honestly speaking, I'm still living that life.

One would think that after the bankruptcy, after the repossession, and after the foreclosure, that I would have changed. But, I didn't.

I still sought out the nicest places to live. I still managed to obtain newer cars to drive. I still tried to look the part of being well-off...knowing, I'm still struggling...still hurting...still living paycheck to paycheck.

No, I was no longer in $250,000 worth of debt...but, there was still no savings. Yeah, I made over $90,000 a year...but, there was still no slush. Maybe, I could have found a part-time job...but, what time would I have had with my young son? And, who could I get to watch him while I worked that second job? But, most importantly, why would I get a second job when I'm going to have to give most of that to a baby-sitter.

Maybe, I could have found a side hustle. Everyone had one of those – back in the days. Everyone...except me.

Immediately after my filing for bankruptcy, I thanked God. I thanked Him for making a way. I thanked Him for not letting me sign with the first or second lawyers that I met with – because had I had done so, I would not have benefited from His plan (to erase *all* of my debt). I thanked Him, for although I didn't see the plan back then, I see it now...and I'm grateful for my lesson of patience.

Immediately after thanking Him, I heard His voice saying..."All I wanted was your time. All I wanted was your obedience. All I wanted was to know that I meant more to you than your earthly possessions...that I meant more to you than those around you...that you loved and appreciated Me for the many things that I have [and continue to do] for you. Will you commit to Me now? I've promised that I will never leave you. But, can you promise to commit to Me?"

I had a moment...standing in front of my bathroom mirror. Hearing His voice, tears began to flow from my eyes, down my face, down my neck, touching my heart. I began realizing – at that very moment – the truth that was being spoken. I had esteemed myself so high all of those years, letting my pride convince me that it was I – me, myself and I – who got me to where I was – professionally. That it was I (and my planning) that got me the nice homes, the nice cars, the furniture and clothes, etc. That is was my skills that led those employers to requesting me...to hiring me. That it was I and my money that helped all of those people in need.

My, how foolish...how foolish I was!

The scripture surely states: Whoever exalts himself [with haughtiness and empty pride] shall be humbled (brought low), and whoever humbles himself [whoever has a modest opinion of himself and behaves accordingly] shall be raised to honor. (Matthew 23:12)

I was humbled to a level of brokenness...because I had exalted myself, instead of recognizing and exalting the One who made it all possible.

I recall going on a trip to my church's annual Women's Retreat. I can vividly remember how *broken* I was. I was so emotional. I was a wreck. I had just filed for bankruptcy. I had just heard God's message. And, I was remorseful. It pained me to know that I caused all of this turmoil upon myself. It pained me to know that I neglected and disregarded the One and only Source that kept me going. It hurt. I hurt.

The retreat was needed that weekend...as it really presented an opportunity for my eyes to be opened. It was the birthday of one of my church elders, and I remember not having any money to buy her a gift. I used to always be able to buy birthday gifts. I was already in attendance at that retreat on borrowed money...but, to not have cash to spend like I wanted to really hurt. I thought to myself, since me and this lady are going to the store (and she's hungry), maybe me buying her lunch and a card will bring a smile to her face. But, then I began tearing up. Because it hurt. A $4 chicken meal and a $2 card...and that was *all* I could buy her. That hurt.

But, I got them for her...explaining that it was all I could do for her birthday at that time. She understood, and kept insisting that I keep my money. But, my pride wouldn't let me. "Please, at least let me do this." I kept asking.

Later that day, I was sitting alone in the Hotel courtyard...feeling sorry for myself. Still in a lot of pain. And, to my surprise, this same lady comes outside and asks to sit with me.

It's almost as if God Himself sent her there. Well, actually, I know it was God that sent her there, because I needed a reality check. Because I needed to be kicked in the rear for saying I was remorseful and understanding of God's will; but, yet, still allowing my pride to consume me. The evil one really knows how to attack you. And, he was doing a good job...until God spoke to me through this well-admired elder.

She mentioned the word, "broken." And, said, that God had to break me, in order for me to wake up and see Who was *really* in charge of my life. I couldn't awaken myself. I couldn't provide for myself. I couldn't open doors of opportunity for myself. I couldn't make ways out of no ways for myself. I couldn't do anything for myself...that God didn't first give me the power to do.

I had to be broken to finally be able to take note to His power...His mercies...His favor upon my life. I had to be broken to finally be able to see that in spite of how the situation looked and/or felt, He was still right there by my side. That, although I considered my situation to be horrific; it wasn't as horrifying as it could have been. His favor was still upon my life. I hadn't lost my job...I was still making more than, if not close to most two-income families...neither me or my family were starving or out on the streets begging...I was blessed with family and friends who cared enough to help, even when my pride was trying to prevent them. Yeah, His favor was still upon my life.

I could have very well lost my mind during this time. Out of all of the things I went through, this moment in my life has got to be one of the hardest. Yeah, I've been violated...yeah, I've been abused...yeah, I've been mistreated...yeah, I've even been disliked. But, nothing has broken my spirit down to this level before.

I was thankful for the conversation that I had with that elder. She was quite instrumental in my spiritual growth...and, I thanked God for using her – on that day – to reach out to me.

I realized that all I had, I had because of God. My promotions...were because of Him. My homes...were because of Him. My cars...were because of Him. My health...was because of Him. Everything I have...is because of Him. I had to learn to let go. I had to learn (because of my pride) what it felt like to lose something, which – at that time – was a SUV that I loved so dearly. A brand-new SUV...that He blessed me with, but that He also took away. He took away what I put before Him. He took away what I valued more than Him. He took away...what I thought made me happy...just so I could see, that without Him, I would have nothing...just so I could see that when I allow myself to let other things – whether it be people, finances or possessions – take precedence over or before Him, how quickly He could take those things away. It is written that God is a jealous God. He's not only jealous of you having other

Gods, but, he's also jealous of other things and/or people that we place before Him.

As our maker – the beginning and the end, we owe Him everything... because in many ways, He's given us what no other man or material possession can ever give – life and life more abundantly.

I didn't realize how real His promises to fulfill all of my needs (f I just trusted in Him) were. It was proven to me just how little faith I actually had...in Him. I started losing things...and almost lost my mind during this phase of my life; and, mostly because I had neglected to recognize and appreciate the One who had taken such great care of me. I neglected to trust in His Word, His promises, His truths. I couldn't see past my current situation to know that all was happening, according to His plan. I couldn't see behind my blinders that He was still there in the midst of my troubles...that He was waiting for me to call upon Him...that He was waiting for me to see that I needed Him, because me, myself and little ol' I didn't really have the power I thought I had.

He allowed the evil one to speak death unto me for so long...until I had gotten to a point of true despair. I actually began believing that God had turned His back on me...that God was so mad at me for getting divorced that He was going to punish me until death. I pained for so long that one day, God hushed the evil one, saying, "That's enough."

During my conversation with that elder, it hit me. I finally realized that instead of crying and feeling sorry for myself, I should have been on my knees, praying to and praising God's holy name. I should have been thanking Him for having mercy upon me to only have taken my car; because, He could have very well taken my life, my sons' lives, my job, my sanity. I realized I needed to focus on getting my relationship back right with Him. I needed to concentrate on building the things that mattered most...my faith in and my obedience to...God.

So, after coming back from that Women's Retreat and having received a revelation from that elder, I could finally see where it was I went wrong. Because I had become so prideful (by thinking that "I" was the reason for all that I had), He had to break me...and broke me, He did.

Now, my tears were not because I lost my car, but because I had turned away from the One source that was always there for me. Like a child who had regretfully upset their parents, I was so remorseful... and so sorry...that I practically begged for His forgiveness.

I immediately started placing all of my trust in God, whether I could see a light at the end of the tunnel or not. I started placing all of my hope in God, giving it all over to Him, understanding that it all belonged to Him anyway.

I stopped caring about money...and, how those bills were going to get paid...because I remembered His Words..."therefore I say unto you, Take no thought for your life, what ye shall eat, or what ye shall drink...behold the fowls of the air; for they sow not, neither do they reap, nor gather into barns; yet, your heavenly Father feedeth them. Are ye not much better than they?" (Matthew 6:25-26)

I began seeing changes all around me. Yeah, I had a 10-year old car to drive, but it was dependable and in the two years that I had it, it never broke down. Yeah, I was still wearing five- to eight-year old clothes, but never did I lose one string of thread on those clothes. In under a month's time, I began seeing ways made out of no ways.

When I needed shoes, He had someone give me several pairs. When I wanted perfume, He had someone give me bottles. When I needed my hair done, He had someone perform a $200 job for free. When I needed food on my table, He had someone fill my refrigerator. When I needed gas in my tank, He had someone to fill that tank. I could go on and on with the works that He was performing (through others); but, that would take another year to write.

All I know is that He promised to never leave me and to never forsake me; and, because He's proven this time and time again, I know – now – that I have absolutely nothing to worry about. He promised that if I take all to Him in prayer, that He would handle it. So, even though I was still living paycheck to paycheck, I knew that some way, somehow, God would still make a way.

Sometimes you have to be made to see that everything on this earth belongs to God, including the money you make. So, if He's blessed you with that job to make it, you should already know He can bless you more if and when you remain faithful to Him while having it. Again, it's just money. And, your God is the richest there is. There is no recession in His book...or His vocabulary...so, you have nothing to worry about. But, remember, that in which you give (sow), you will also receive (reap). Sow sparingly...and you will reap sparingly (2 Corinthians 9:6).

On a similar note, I failed to mention how often I used to complain about having to work as hard I had for everything that I have, while others seemed to be given break after break; but, now, I've come to realize – from all of my years of having to work (and work hard), that it was for my own good. I can see (just from watching others) that had God handed me everything on a silver platter...that had God not let me experience and go through these storms...that had God not lowered me into a spirit of brokenness, I would not know and/or be able to fully appreciate His goodness. Nor, would I be able to testify to you and others about how faithful He is...in all of His wondrous works.

I can't see and don't know my life's planned course; but, because I know He does, I have come to understand that that is the reason I need to place my complete trust in Him...that I need to always remember that He will never lead me where His grace will not follow. I understand that all things happen for a reason...and, all for our own good. Every struggle and every trial is meant to serve as a lesson.

I'm still learning. I still have a lot of growing to do…especially in better managing my money; but, at least I now know from where comes my help.

ROUND NINE:
TOUCHED

God. Who is He,
and what exactly can He do?
Would you know how to respond
if He began speaking to you?
All my life, I'd gone to church,
only to hear the words spoken.
Never once thought I'd need Him...
so, what reason would I go searching?
Heard of the 10 commandments...
I probably followed one or two.
And that's only because I felt
those were the right things to do.
Twenty-eight years had gone by
before I finally had a revelation.
After giving birth to my youngest son,
I finally saw the bigger picture.
To look at how perfect every inch
of his little body was...
I thanked God right then and there
for peeling the shades off of my eyes.
Looking back over my past,
I could see His works all around me.
Everything that I went through,
it was Him that kept me moving.

'Footprints' was my story;
I could relate to every word.
Touched by His spirit,
I finally believed that God was real.
Started praying, going to church,
hanging around Christian mentors.
I was proud of the relationship
that I was finally building with Him.
Found it amazing how His Word
was proven true every time.
He said to try Him, and to trust Him,
and He would always be right there.
When I thought there was no way,
when I felt I'd hit a brick wall...
God always showed His favor
whenever I made that call.
Bills were stacking up,
no food was in the refrigerator.
But, out of nowhere,
checks were cleared and food was on the table.
I cannot tell you how very happy I am
to have a friend as good as He.
He's my provider, protector, healer, lover...
all that I need Him to be.
Not one has come close...
not one can even compare.
I thank God for being the head of my life...
no one else should I fear.

Used to try to complain about the things
I wanted and did not have.
Until He showed me how to be happy
with things He'd blessed me with.
Used to always whine about not having
a decent man in my life.
Until He made me realize I, too,
had things I needed to get right.
Used to think I needed a nice car
and plenty of fancy clothes.
Until He humbled me into seeing
that those things will, too, get old.
The only thing that remains
constant is His undying love for me.
Got me claiming to the world
of just how real God is to me.
Some could never understand
the way I chose to live my life...
Why I chose to be Not Like Most,
why I always tried to do what was right.
"Keep it movin" was my motto;
I refused to let the devil win.
He's on my back all the time...
but, in front of me is my best friend.
Always there to comfort me,
always there to protect and lead...
A force so strong and powerful,
one name was all I needed.

'Father'...that was and
is all I said, cried, and screamed.
And, to the rescue He was there...
to assist and/or help me.
Never had to worry...
all my trust I put into Him.
Then, watched as He unfolded
each and every blessing.
For those who have yet to experience
the true joys of knowing Him,
I pray for a quick revealing
to show just how magnificent God is.
Once you begin to put Him first
and make all efforts to keep Him there,
He will quickly give you peace;
His Word will never fail.
No lies will His mouth speak;
no stories will He make up.
No talks behind your back;
never empty will be your cup.
Take it from someone who
has had a real first-hand experience...
There's no greater love,
and definitely no greater gift...
than that of the Most High –
He is to be adored forever.
Cause only He can give you peace
and a joy like no other.

**Let your light so shine before men,
that they may see your good works,
and glorify your Father which is in heaven.**

Matthew 5:16 (KJV)

Jesus loves me. This I know...
for the Bible tells me so.
Little ones to Him belong;
they are weak, but He is strong.
Yes...Jesus loves me.
Yes...Jesus loves me.
Yes...Jesus loves me...
for the Bible tells me so.

So many people call themselves believers...but, very few actually are.

I didn't go to church much while living at home with my mother; but, the years I spent with my grandmother, every Sunday I had to be there. Sometimes the pastor would say things that made sense and that I could understand; but, I found that unless he was hoopin' and hollerin', I wasn't catching a word that was coming out of his mouth. Most of the time that would be because boredom was not something I handled well...so, I would always look for distractions...like checking out that cute guy on the other side of the church, whom I caught glancing at me. At other times, I wasn't listening because I didn't understand the messages that the pastors were trying to relay.

I attended church often; but, I never took my attendance seriously. Nor, did I take my belief in God seriously. As a matter of fact, in my younger years, I found myself constantly doubting that there even was a God.

You see...I can vividly remember – as a young adult – thinking of all of the negative things that I had gone through, all of the hurtful things that I had to endure, all of the turmoil that I had to put up with...year after year, occasion after occasion. And, along with those thoughts, I also recalled frequently wondering just where God was during those times. It seemed like with each passing year, I would have storm after storm, trial after trial, tribulation after painful tribulation [including things that I haven't even mentioned in this book], that all left me questioning God's love for me.

Where was He when I was being treated like a red-headed step-child? Where was He when I was being molested and raped? Where was He when my mom was being beat on? Where was He when my grandfather lost his desire to live? Where was He when my son's father elected to not be a father? Where was He when I was being disrespected and constantly disregarded in my marriage? Where was He when my enemies were surrounding me, attacking me? Where was He when I was losing my sanity over my finances and other burdens? Where was He when I laid crying in my bed night after night, not knowing which path to take or which road to follow? Or, better yet, why did He allow all of those things to happen to *me...*if *He loved me so much?*

It always seemed as if I was given the short end of the stick...like everyone else was more loved than me...like everyone else was prospering and benefitting from His blessings...except for me.

As a child, and even through adulthood, I used to find myself crying when it came time to pray to God, to talk about God, or even to talk *to* God. Tears would literally flow from my eyes, as if it pained me to say His name. I used to always wonder what those tears were about. What is it that makes me cry at just the thought of Him?

It was just recently revealed through an associate that those tears were and still are my spirit's way of speaking to God. It was revealed to me that I had been touched by God – long before *I* knew Him. That somebody somewhere prayed for me, even when I didn't know how to pray for myself. That God loved somebody so much that He granted their wish of saving me...protecting me...having mercy upon me...but, most of all, He granted their wish for Him to never take His hands off of me.

But, not knowing that back then, I had actually stopped praying...one, because I didn't want to cry; and, two, because I felt like He wasn't listening anyway. I called on Him so many nights when I was being molested and raped...only for Him to allow me to continue going through it. I called on Him so many nights when my mom was getting into fights with her boyfriends…only for Him to allow her to continue going through it. I called on Him so many nights when I laid there worrying about how this bill or that bill was going to get paid…only for Him to allow me to continue going through it. I called on Him so many times when I bared frequent pains from stomach issues…only for Him to allow me to continue going through it. For so long, I used to think that He had taken His hands off of me…that He had forgotten all about me…that He was, perhaps, too busy to even care about me.

Not knowing that these things were happening, according to His will. Not knowing that He would eventually answer my prayers…but, in His timing, and not mine. I was always looking for immediate gratification…an immediate rescue. But, I had to learn that my time table didn't always correspond with His.

It took years for me to come to this realization.

I've noted to you over the previous eight chapters of how He's brought me through each and every situation. But, I would not have even been able to fully tell my story, had He not – first – revealed Himself and His love to me.

In each of the situations outlined in this book, my spirit was constantly being tried, tested…beaten, even. The devil tried all he could to kill me…to destroy me…but, through it all, I had a friend – in the midst – who never took His hands off of me…and who protected and shielded me.

…and, who, still – to this day, is keeping me…close to His bosom.

Everyone has a free will to believe in who or what they want. Everyone has free will to do what and how they want. But, with all, everyone has a force that they will have to answer to…and give account to for everything that they've done in their lives…whether good or bad.

You've probably already noticed that this book is centered around one God. The God in which I believe in. The God in which I trust in. The God in which all of my hope lies in.

You see, no matter what you're going through, no matter what storm is brewing around you, no matter how tall that mountain looks, you have to remember that God is bigger than any situation. Even if your faith is the size of a mustard seed, God can work that miracle for you. God can change your circumstances. God can make even your enemies bow before you.

All it takes is prayer...and a belief that He can; but, more importantly, it takes prayer, and your faith that He will. You see, God is not a forceful God. He is a loving God...waiting with open arms for you to come to Him...for you to call on Him...and, not just because you need help; but, because you love and revere Him.

He created each of us...from His love. He's kept each of us...with His love. And, He's delivered each of us...by His love. Our problem is we get too busy and/or become neglectful in recognizing His love, His blessings, His mercies...we get too busy to even remember the little things...like just being thankful that He woke us up this morning...like just being thankful that our home was protected overnight, our kids were awakened and made it safely to and from school, our job hadn't been terminated, our lights are still on, our health hasn't completely failed us.

We are so focused on the issue at hand that we fail to realize that God has it all under control. We get so engrossed with the troubles in our lives that we fail to realize that not only does God already know the ending, but that He can direct us through each and every storm. We get so stressed out over situations and circumstances that we fail to realize that if we just gave it all over to God, those stresses would be removed...because He is...God. He will make a way for you...and, not because He has to...but, because...He loves you. And, all He asks is that you show your faith in Him, that you love and revere Him, and that you remain obedient to Him.

And, that can start as early as childhood.

Like most people, I used to only pray when something bad was happening to me...when a storm was present that I didn't know how to handle...when life was forcing me to go in directions that I had no familiarity with...when circumstances weren't very lending to productive and positive growth. Those times used to be the only times in which I even made time for God.

But, He remained by my side...still.

I became saved right after the birth of my second son. After having prayed (before giving birth) that God would have mercy upon my delivery...that He would allow me to give birth without any major complications...and, that He would breathe life into my unborn child (upon delivery), and allow him or her to be in perfect health. Well, needless to say, all went well...and my son...perfect.

I began crying as I began thanking God for the miracle that He had blessed me with. I couldn't help but to be overjoyed at the sight of my son...I couldn't help but to pay tribute to the One who made it all possible. I told God – then – that I was going to dedicate myself to Him. It didn't happen overnight...but, it did happen.

I started noticing a difference in me from that point forward. No, I wasn't a saint...I didn't live strictly by the Bible...I didn't even - yet - know how to forgive and love everyone, in spite of the pain they caused me...I hadn't - yet - grown to a matured level in Christ, as a means to help lead someone else to Him...but, He remained patient...still.

Patient and understanding.

Even during my talks with Him (around the time of my divorce), I recall being so overwhelmed with fear and remorse that all I could do was ask for His mercy. My spirit had been broken so much that I knew He knew I couldn't go on...that He knew the devil was trying his best to win that battle, and that I was starting to grow weary.

I'm a firm believer that God knows just how much you can handle...and that He would never put more on you than you can. Those statements were proven true...each and every time.

In each of my situations, I had gotten to a breaking point...to a point that I was always fearful of; because, in every situation, I found myself plotting something evil against those who were hurting me. Anytime that I began feeling uneasy about my thoughts and things I was wanting to do, I would immediately begin praying. Although I had only heard of God (through half listening in Church), it was during my lowest times that I actually felt, 'what else do I have to lose?' If God is real, He will deliver me...from this.

And, each and every time...He did.
It may not have been right when I wanted Him to...or felt I needed Him to...but, it was always right on time. Not once have I been incarcerated. Not once have I been admitted into a Psych Ward. Not once have I had to truly act on those ill feelings that I had. Not once have I ever gotten to see that side of me that He's successfully kept buried all of these years.

And, I thank Him for it.

His Light

Felt alone and unwanted,
but God showed himself.
Was tired and worn down,
but God gave me strength.
Felt used and unloved,
but my eyes were often opened...
To see the grace and mercy
that He faithfully showed me.
Was broke and often discouraged
when it came to getting the bills paid.
Tried to do right,
but often found I wasn't perfect.
Didn't have many friends,
but was thankful for the few...
Cause they were vessels used by God
to send His blessings through.
Many misunderstood me,
many never had my back.
But, it sure was nice to find out
that God was always there.

I Thank You, Lord

For Your blood that cleanses me;
for Your word that strengthens me;
for Your love that keeps me, I thank You, Lord.
For being the father I never had;
for being the friend who's always there;
for being the love of my life,
I thank You, Lord.

For my sons and my family;
for my friends and even my enemies;
for every one I've ever met, I thank You, Lord.
For awakening me, for protecting me;
for blessing me with Your favor...
for showing me, for being true to me,
for always remaining faithful...
I thank You, Lord.

There's no one greater,
no one better who could move me like You do...
For You've told and You've shown me
just how much You really love me,
and I thank You, Lord.

If I had just one more wish
before my day to leave this earth
and You asked what would it be,
and just how much is it worth?
I'd say to live in eternity
with my Savior and my God,
and to have that wish come true
I'd gladly give up all...
because I thank You, Lord.

Recoil...

So many people look at me, and although I walk a similar walk as them, and talk a similar talk as them, they recognize that I am not quite like them. There's something different...there's something special...there's something there that only God could have placed there...His light.

I've never been one for many words; but, I have no problems – now – giving witness to His greatness. I've found Him placing people into my life – even if it were for just a moment – that needed ministering to. Mostly young girls and women – who had gone through similar or the same situations that I had. And, even though hearing of their pains made mine resurface, He still used me to give an encouraging Word, and to be a living testimony.

My constant prayer is always that He uses me to bring good to this earth. You see, I understand that we all have a purpose on this earth, and that that purpose has nothing to do with our own selfish goals, motives, etc...but, on the contrary, has everything to do with God's Will being done. What people fail to realize is that their situations are much bigger than what they can see. It's a spiritual battle...one in which you can let the evil one win, or one in which you can let God take and have control over.

As spoken all throughout this book, we all have choices. And, God gives us a choice...to follow, trust in, love and revere Him – the lover of our souls; or, to worship the evil forces on this earth. I chose God...and I know I have, because I can feel Him all around me.

I thought it was funny how when I first heard a particular R&B song that was noting a woman's love for a man, and of how he was everything she needed him to be, and how thankful she was to the Heavens for that man...I immediately thought of God when I heard that song; because He has been that man for me.

So many have said that God was their provider, their healer, their protector, their redeemer, their father, their best friend, their lover, their...everything...but, how many really feel that way? How many *really* believe that? With a belief that stems all the way to their core?

I am a living witness that God is EVERY THING. From the air that you breathe, to the food that you eat, to your protection on the roads, to the covering of your children, to the comforter of your spirit, to the lover of your soul...there's no one greater, no one more powerful, no one more able, no one more trust-worthy, no one more faithful, no one more loving...than our beloved, Most High.

And, you know this, because how many other people do you know that can perform miracles as He did (and still does), and would give their life so that you may have eternal life? We've all said, "I'd die for my kids, my wife, my husband, etc..."; but, not without selfish reasons. Doing it without any selfishness is called, real love.

I don't care how you choose to look at it...and, I'm sorry for those who may be reading this book who don't believe in God; but, my prayer is that you would be touched in a way that will allow God's love to spread amongst, around and within you. My prayer is that your mind is not so closed that you can't receive the Word that's being delivered to you. My prayer is that you will be touched - in some form or fashion – by the words that are being written on these pages.

God has so much love that He truly wants to share it with all. All you have to do is share yourself with Him...to place Him first in your life, so that He can direct your paths...in a much more rewarding direction.

So many people shun Christianity because of all of the so-called rules and regulations that you "have to" follow; but, in reality, Christianity – to me – is all about love, and the spreading of that love. Christianity – to me – is about my personal relationship with God – the Father, the Son

and the Holy Spirit. Christianity – to me – is about my walk, my talk, my growth in He who watches over me – night and day.
To me, Jesus is real. Jesus is alive. Jesus is Lord.

I can't tell you how many times I've personally called upon that name...and how, every time, I got this rush over me that felt like 'fire in my bones.' I can't tell you how many times I've prayed to Him, or in His name, and how many of those prayers have actually gotten answered. I can't tell you how many times I made time to worship and praise Him, to immediately after have a rush of complete joy come over me. I can't tell you how blessed I've been – all of my life, but most importantly, how I am now able to recognize His never-ceasing presence in my life.

I've shared with you on many occasions of how God was always with me – in the midst of my storms...but, I also want you to remember that just like He's been there (and is still there for me), He can be there for you, as well...but, it all depends on your faith...in Him.

Do you believe in Him? Do you trust Him? Will you give yourself to Him...knowing that you belong to Him anyway? Will you depend on Him to take care of you, to protect you? Will you call on Him when you're in need? Will you praise Him and show Him how much you appreciate His presence in your life? Will you tell someone else of His goodness? Will you be a witness to His works in your life?

Will you love the One...who first loved you?

I asked you those questions, because they are critical to your growth...critical to your walk with Him. So many people claim to believe in God, claim to trust in Him, claim to worship Him...but, let something happen, and they fall completely apart. That's not having faith in Him!

I have family members and friends who can come to me right now about issues and/or problems that they're having in their lives...and, as soon as I mention God, they try to quickly change the subject; yet, they say they believe in Him. As soon as I advise of them doing the right thing, they want to turn their noses up, and treat me as if I was judging them...when in actuality, I wasn't. I was merely trying to help them build and strengthen their own faith...by sharing His truth and His Word.

So many look at me and wonder just how it is I can be where I am? Just why it is I look at life so differently...just why it is I refuse to associate with drama and confusion...just why it is I've learned to accept death and have already prepared my own obituary...just why it is I become overjoyed with the simplest of God's blessings, and even more so with the grandest – like when His Spirit speaks [in tongues] through me. Many don't understand just why it is I don't get as stressed as most over the simplest of things.

Notice I said *as* stressed, because just like you, I'm still human. I'm still prone to becoming fearful of something...but, it's those times when I have to hasten to my "closet", remembering His Word, and praying steadfastly for His help. It is in those times that I regain my strength and am able to continue standing, instead of fainting. It is in those times that I have to remember to "let go and let God."

I know, for some of you, that's easier said than done...but, there's no perfection without practice. So, practice it. Get serious about your walk with God. Get serious about your belief in God. Please heed my advice and stop playing with your life and your relationship with Him...because, believe it or not, your days are numbered. Only God knows when your last moment of life will be on this earth...but, only you can control where you go when that moment comes.

The earth is being destroyed...and everything in it will be destroyed... but, will you live? Will you be one of the chosen ones that God raises up? Will your name be written in that Book of Life?

Now, I'm asking these questions out of a genuine concern for my people...for God's people. Many of you, I'm sure I don't personally know; but, through God's love, I love and care about you the same, as if I did.

I don't claim to be perfect...but, I'm trying. I don't claim to be where I need to be...but, I'm striving. I am a woman...who has gone grazed by many bullets (storms of life); but, by the grace of God...

I am a **woman**...

who has **survived**.

**I sought the Lord, and he heard me,
and delivered me from all my fears.**

Psalm 34:4 (KJV)

REFERENCES

Domestic
Violence Help: **NATIONAL DOMESTIC VIOLENCE HOTLINE**
Website: http://www.ndvh.org/get-help/
Phone: 1-800-799-SAFE (7233)
Anonymous and Confidential Help – 24/7

Child Abuse Help: **NATIONAL CHILDHOOD ABUSE HOTLINE**
Website: http://childhelp.org/get_help
Phone: 1-800-799-SAFE (7233)
Free and Anonymous Help – 24/7

Sexual
Assault Help   **NATIONAL SEXUAL ASSUALT HOTLINE**
Rape, Abuse and Incest National Network
Website: http://www.rainn.org/get-help/
Phone: 1-800-656-HOPE
Free and Confidential Help – 24/7

Teen
Pregnancy Help   **NATIONAL TEEN PREGNANCY HOTLINE**
Website: http://www.pregnancycenters.org/
Phone: 1-800-395-HELP
Confidential Help – 24/7

Bankruptcy/
Credit Help   **NATIONAL FOUNDATION FOR CREDIT COUNSELING**
Website: http://www.nfcc.org/
Phone: 1-800-388-2227

About The Author

Bodie Quinette, a Georgia native, is a creative writer who has always had a passion for poetry, art, music and spirituality. Known for her compassionate, but 'keeping it real' nature, Bodie's journey of dealing with the continuous stresses of life and living have remarkably transformed her into the spiritually motivated individual she is today. With each and every storm she has been blessed to overcome, Bodie has gained a deeper awareness and understanding of God's presence in her life, and is not ashamed to let the world know from where her strength, wisdom and blessings come.

"Bullet Proof" is a personal testimony written to encourage and/or help the hurt, deprived, confused, shattered and lost. May all who decide to take this journey with Bodie be spiritually touched and Heavenly blessed...as God, Himself, has blessed her.

THE SOLID FOUNDATION GROUP

MORE GREAT BOOKS!
ORDER FORM

Mail along with payment to: **P.O. Box 1483   Smyrna, GA 30081**

Name

Address

City

State   Zip

Book		Qty	Total
	Bullet Proof by Bodie Quinette *Genre: Self-Help/Motivational* Cost: $15.95/each*		$
	The Cartel's Daughter Unedited: ***Raw and Uncut!*** by Carmine *Genre: Crime/Thriller/Urban* Cost: $14.99/each*		$
	*SHIPPING & HANDLING: *Four dollars ($4) must be included for **each** book ordered.* *Please allow 7-10 business days for delivery.*		$
	TOTAL ENCLOSED		$

Acceptable Forms of Payment: *Money orders or U.S. bank issued checks made payable to **The Solid Foundation Group**. Please do not send cash.*

Visit our website for a complete listing of books published by TSFG and/or to order online:
WWW.THESOLIDFOUNDATIONGROUP.COM

CPSIA information can be obtained
at www.ICGtesting.com
Printed in the USA
LVOW10s1913210517
535301LV00001B/1/P